Dive into Reading

The East Hampton Library Children's Fair

A gift from

Library Lover
Hannah Bloom

D0845666

YOUTH COPING WITH TEEN PREGNANCY

Growing Up Fast

HELPING YOUTH WITH MENTAL, PHYSICAL, AND SOCIAL CHALLENGES

Title List

YOUTH COPING WITH TEEN
PREGNANCY

Growing Up
Fast

by Heather Docalavich
and Phyllis Livingston

Mason Crest Publishers
Philadelphia

Mason Crest Publishers Inc.
370 Reed Road
Broomall, Pennsylvania 19008
(866) MCP-BOOK (toll free)
www.masoncrest.com

Copyright © 2008 by Mason Crest Publishers. All rights reserved. No part of this publication may be reproduced or transmitted in any form or by any means, electronic or mechanical, including photocopying, recording, taping, or any information storage and retrieval system, without permission from the publisher.

First printing

1 2 3 4 5 6 7 8 9 10

ISBN 978-1-4222-0133-6 (series)

Library of Congress Cataloging-in-Publication Data

Docalavich, Heather.
  Youth coping with teen pregnancy : growing up fast / by Heather Docalavich and Phyllis Livingston.
      p. cm. — (Helping youth with mental, physical, and social challenges)
  Includes bibliographical references and index.
  ISBN-13: 978-1-4222-0134-3
  1. Teenage mothers. 2. Teenage pregnancy. 3. Single mothers. I. Livingston, Phyllis, 1957– II. Title.
HQ759.4.D63 2008
306.874'32—dc22
                                          2006027115

Interior pages produced by
Harding House Publishing Service, Inc.
www.hardinghousepages.com
Interior design by MK Bassett-Harvey.
Cover design by MK Bassett-Harvey.
Cover Illustration by Keith Rosko.
Printed in the Hashemite Kingdom of Jordan.

The creators of this book have made every effort to provide accurate information, but it should not be used as a substitute for the help and services of trained professionals.

SEP 2 2 2009

Contents

Introduction

We are all people first, before anything else. Our shared humanity is more important than the impressions we give to each other by how we look, how we learn, or how we act. Each of us is worthy simply because we are all part of the human race. Though we are all different in many ways, we can celebrate our differences as well as our similarities.

In this book series, you will read about many young people with various special needs that impact their lives in different ways. The disabilities are not *who* the people are, but the disabilities are an important characteristic of each person. When we recognize that we all have differing needs, we can grow toward greater awareness and tolerance of each other. Just as important, we can learn to accept our differences.

Not all young people with a disability are the same as the persons in the stories. But you will learn from these stories how a special need impacts a young person, as well as his or her family and friends. The story will help you understand differences better and appreciate how differences make us all stronger and better.

—*Cindy Croft, M.A.Ed.*

Did you know that as many as 8 percent of teens experience anxiety or depression, and as many as 70 to 90 percent will use substances such as alcohol or illicit drugs at some time? Other young people are living with life-threatening diseases including HIV infection and cancer, as well as chronic psychiatric conditions such as bipolar disease and schizophrenia. Still other teens have the challenge of being "different" from peers because they are intellectually gifted, are from another culture, or have trouble controlling their behavior or socializing with others. All youth with challenges experience additional stresses compared to their typical peers. The good news is that there are many resources and supports available to help these young people, as well as their friends and families.

The stories contained in each book of this series also contain factual information that will enhance your own understanding of the particular condition being presented. If you or someone you know is struggling with a similar condition or experience, this series can give you important information about where and how you can get help. After reading these stories, we hope that you will be more open to the differences you encounter in your peers and more willing to get to know others who are "different."

—*Carolyn Bridgemohan, M.D.*

Chapter 1
Getting the News

Holly knew something was wrong. She had been trying to ignore it for several weeks, but changes were taking place in her body that were becoming more and more difficult to dismiss as simply being overtired or having a bout with the flu. She hadn't felt like herself for weeks. She knew she needed to start looking at some very scary possibilities.

Holly also knew she and her boyfriend Scott hadn't been as careful as they should have been. When they had first started having sex, Scott always used a condom. As time went on though, Holly and Scott had found themselves in situations where they didn't always have a condom available. Scott had always said not to worry about it: so long as he "pulled out," he insisted, everything would be fine.

But Holly's period was now nearly a month late—and somehow she knew that everything was not fine. She was nauseated all the time, and sometimes she had to dart into the girls' bathroom between classes to throw up. Her breasts were so swollen and tender it seemed like torture to wear a bra, and she had no energy to do anything short of going to school and coming home and going to bed.

Holly's health teacher kept a stack of pamphlets near the classroom door with information about a local family planning clinic. One day at the end of class, Holly took one on her way out the door. She asked Scott to go with her to the clinic later that afternoon.

"What do I need to go to some stupid clinic for?" He avoided Holly's eyes as he spoke. "There's nothing wrong with you. You know I pulled out whenever we didn't use a condom. This is all in your head. I'm sick of talking about it. If you want to go, then do it! But don't drag me along." Scott slung his book bag over his shoulders and slouched off toward the school parking lot.

The next morning Holly got dressed as usual and said good-bye to her mother and younger brother as if she were heading off to school. Instead, she caught a bus that would take her downtown to the family planning clinic. She didn't have any trouble finding the building. A handful of men and women with picket signs were marching back and forth in front of the building. From what she could read on the signs, Holly could see that they were protesting the clinic because it provided counseling and referral services for abortion. This scared her a little, but Holly knew she had to do something; this was probably the best place for her to go for help. Taking a deep breath and squaring her shoulders, Holly walked past the protesters and through the clinic door.

Holly's first impression of the clinic was that it looked pretty much the same as any other doctor's office she had been to. The empty waiting area had chairs and low tables piled with magazines. A table for children stood in the corner stacked with blocks and small toys.

The brochure she had from school had said "no appointments necessary," but now it seemed like maybe she should have called ahead. As if sensing her dilemma, a friendly looking older woman poked her head out past the glass of the window that separated the office from the waiting room and asked, "How can I help you, dear?"

"Well . . . um, I'm not sure. I . . . uh, I think there's a chance I might be pregnant." Saying the words out loud for the first time made Holly squirm.

"All right then." The woman didn't seem shocked or even surprised. "I'll just need you to take these forms and fill them out for me. As you probably know, we offer free preg-nancy testing here. We also provide routine family planning and gynecological services on a sliding scale, based on your ability to pay. Do you have a job?"

Holly cleared her throat. "No, ma'am."

"Well, that's fine then. We'll go ahead and get you set up for your pregnancy test, and then you'll go in to see our nurse practitioner. She'll probably want to test you for sex-ually transmitted diseases as well. These are tests we also offer for free. After that, depending on the results of your pregnancy test, you'll visit with one of our counselors who can talk with you about your options if you *are* pregnant—or help you choose a reliable method of birth control if the test is negative. Just go ahead and fill out those papers for me and we'll get started."

Holly did as she was told and then returned her papers to the receptionist. She was called into the back of the office after just a few minutes. They had her catch some urine in a plastic cup and then sit in a chair next to the counter. She watched as the nurse used a dropper to place three drops of urine onto the plastic strip. Her head began to swim as she saw a blue "plus" sign appear almost instantly.

"What was the date of your last period?" the nurse asked. Holly gave her the date, and the nurse took out a little card-board wheel. "Well, you are definitely pregnant. According to your period, about eight weeks pregnant. Let's go ahead and get you in for a pelvic exam with our nurse practitioner. She'll also take some cultures and some blood to test for any sexually transmitted diseases, and then we'll send you in to talk with one of the counselors."

The nurse led Holly to a tiny exam room dominated by a large examining table with stirrups for the patient's feet. Nearby, Holly saw a silver tray with an assortment of instruments and a tube of lubricant. Holly began to shake. All of a sudden, she realized this was the first time she had visited a doctor's office without her mother. Before she had time to do or say anything, Holly felt the nausea rise from her belly; without warning she threw up her morning orange juice all over the exam room floor.

"Not to worry, accidents happen." The nurse didn't look upset or grossed out. "Just sit down and take it easy, okay?"

"I'm so sorry." Holly gulped back tears.

"Don't worry," the nurse repeated. "You have enough on your mind today. Just sit down and I'll be back with a can of ginger ale for you and someone with a mop to clean up the mess. When you feel steady on your feet again, there is a gown on the exam table. Take off everything from the waist down and put the gown on. But wait until you feel a little more steady. There's no rush!"

A few minutes later Holly gratefully accepted her small can of ginger ale and a packet of saltine crackers. As she sipped the ginger ale, the queasiness in her stomach began to subside. Still wishing that her mom could have been here with her, Holly changed into the gown and lay down on the examining table.

Holly made it through her pelvic exam and blood tests without registering much of what was happening or being said to her. The nurse practitioner mentioned something about her uterus being the "appropriate size" for her expected due date. Nothing seemed real to Holly as she lay on the examining table; all she could think was that she was supposed to be in English class with all her friends, not in some strange clinic having a nurse feel her uterus and test her for syphilis.

Once the exam was finished, Holly lay on the exam table for several long moments, completely overwhelmed by what she had learned. How would she tell Scott? How would she tell her family and friends? Would she tell her family and friends at all? Maybe something would happen to the baby and she could just go on with her life like this never happened.

She wasn't very healthy; her doctor was always complaining that she was underweight. Plus, she and Scott had been drinking at parties on the weekends. That was supposed to be bad for babies, right? Maybe this whole nightmare would just go away on its own. Holly climbed off the table and began getting dressed, suddenly feeling a little hopeful that somewhere in all of this someone had made a mistake.

Just then another nurse poked her head through the door of the exam room. "Holly, are you dressed? The counselor is ready to talk to you now."

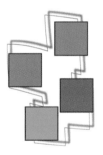

Sex and Pregnancy

Sex and pregnancy are two words that go together. The only 100 percent accurate method of birth control is **abstinence**. That's why the decision to have sex is one young adults should think through carefully.

Having sex is a life-changing experience. Some teenagers choose to have sex, while others wait. Some teenagers don't use contraception and get pregnant, and others get pregnant even using contraception. Pregnant teenagers have difficult decisions to make. Some teenagers choose to have abortions, others give up their babies for adoption, and some choose to become parents. Before having sex, a person should understand the risks and consequences of these life-changing decisions. This understanding begins with knowledge of how the reproductive system works.

The Male Body

The reproduction system is a set of organs that make it possible for a couple to reproduce. The sex organs of a male are different than a female's, and each organ has a different function. A male's reproductive organs are located both outside and inside his body. The **genitals** are the penis and the scrotum. The penis is made of spongy tissue and blood vessels. It is shaped like a tube and consists of two parts: the shaft, which becomes hard during erections; and the rounded tip, called the glans (sometimes called the tip or the head). The penis contains the urethra, the channel that carries urine out of the body. In the process called ejaculation, semen is released through the urethra. (Urine cannot come out during an ejaculation.) Also, the penis is a source of sexual pleasure.

The scrotum is the flexible bag of wrinkly skin that covers and protects the two testicles or testes. In order to produce sperm, the testicles must be kept at a temperature just below body temperature, so the testicles normally hang away from the body. During **puberty**, males start making sex cells. The hormone testosterone is released and causes sperm cells to mature inside the testicles.

Each testicle is connected to a small tube-like structure called the epididymis. Sperm cells travel from each testicle, through the epididymis to the vas deferens. The two vas deferens, sometimes called

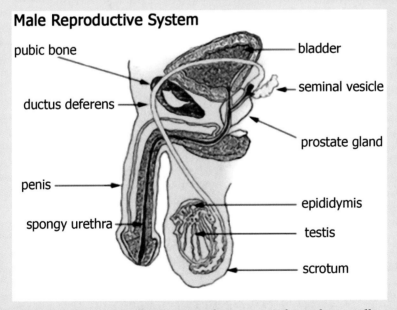

Male Reproductive System

pubic bone — bladder

ductus deferens — seminal vesicle

— prostate gland

penis —

epididymis

spongy urethra —

testis

scrotum

During puberty males begin to produce sperm, the male sex cells. Millions of sperm are produced in the testicles every day.

sperm ducts, are narrow tubes that deliver sperm from the testicles to the seminal vesicles for storage until ejaculation. Each tube starts at the epididymis and winds all the way to the urethra. The two seminal vesicles and the prostate gland produce fluids that combine with the sperm to create a mixture called semen. The urethra is part of the urinary system. This tube carries urine from the bladder, to the penis, and out through the opening of the penis. The urethra is also the passageway for semen. As sperm travel, they mature and become able to fertilize a female's egg. The sperm travel along in the fluids to and through the urethra.

Once a male's body begins to produce sperm, he will continue to produce sperm for the rest of his life. Millions of sperm are produced each day. If not ejaculated, the body absorbs the sperm.

The Female Body

Like the male reproductive system, some of the female's sex organs are on the outside of the body, while others are located inside the body. The breasts are located on the upper part of the body. These organs provide nourishment for babies. They contain the mammary glands, which produce breast milk during and after pregnancy.

The whole area of soft skin between a female's legs is called the vulva. The vulva covers the entire genital area of the labia, the clitoris, the opening to the urethra, and the opening to the vagina. The labia are two sets of soft folds of skin inside the vulva. They cover the inner parts of the vulva—the clitoris, the opening to the urethra, and the opening to the vagina. The clitoris is a small mound of skin about the size of a pea, and its purpose is sexual pleasure. The urethra is not one of the female's sex organs. It is a tube with a small opening through which urine leaves the body. The vagina is a passageway between the uterus and the outside of the female body. Also, the vagina is the passage for the menstrual flow and the opening for sexual intercourse. The opening to the vagina is bigger than the opening to the urethra.

Inside the female abdomen are two ovaries, two fallopian tubes, the uterus, and the vagina. One ovary is on each side of the uterus. The ovaries contain a

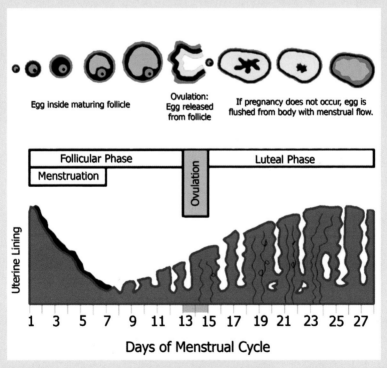

Egg inside maturing follicle

Ovulation: Egg released from follicle

If pregnancy does not occur, egg is flushed from body with menstrual flow.

Follicular Phase

Menstruation

Ovulation

Luteal Phase

Uterine Lining

1 3 5 7 9 11 13 15 17 19 21 23 25 27

Days of Menstrual Cycle

Females are born with millions of sex cells, eggs, in each ovary. After a girl reaches puberty, one egg matures and is released during her monthly menstrual cycle. From this point on, pregnancy is possible.

female's sex cells—also called eggs or ova; a single egg is called an ovum. Females are born with millions of eggs in each ovary, but the eggs do not begin maturing until puberty. The two fallopian tubes are channels that lead from the ovaries to the uterus. One end of each tube almost touches an ovary, while the other end of each tube is connected to the uterus.

The uterus is the place in which a developing baby grows for about nine months until it is ready to be born. Sometimes called the womb, the uterus stretches as the fetus grows. The uterus is made of strong muscles and is hollow inside. It is about the size and shape of a small upside-down pear and is connected to both fallopian tubes and the inside end of the vagina.

The vagina is the passageway from the uterus to the outside of the female body. A baby travels through the vagina when it is ready to be born. The vagina is also the passageway through which a small amount of blood, other fluids, and tissue leave the uterus, about once a month. This small amount of normal bleeding is called menstruation or "having a period" and begins when a girl reaches puberty. The vagina is also the place where the penis fits during sexual intercourse.

The cervix is a small opening located in the lower part of the uterus. It extends into the top of the vagina. This opening is the entrance to the uterus and fallopian tubes, so sperm travel up through the cervix. The cervix is the exit from the uterus for menstrual flow.

Ovulation

At the start of puberty, the ovaries begin to produce the hormones estrogen and progesterone. About once a month, the ovaries begin to release a single mature egg. In her life, a female will release about four hundred to five hundred eggs. This periodic release of a mature egg from an ovary is called ovulation. At about the same time every month, when an egg is released from one of the ovaries, it is swept into one of the fallopian tubes, where it begins to travel to the uterus. If the egg is not fertilized, it is discharged from the body as part of the menstrual flow. Sperm can live up to five days and the egg lives twenty-four hours. This means a woman can get pregnant after intercourse, a few days before ovulation, or a day after.

Reproduction

As soon as a female's ovaries have begun to release eggs, she can become pregnant if she has sexual intercourse. Sexual intercourse is the sexual joining of two individuals, and it happens when a male's erect penis enters the female's vagina. When the male ejaculates or releases semen into the female's vagina, millions of sperm travel through the cervix and up a fallopian tube. If an egg is present in the fallopian tube, the egg can become fertilized. Conception is the moment the sperm fertilizes the egg. The fertilized egg then travels through the fallopian tube, into the uterus, and attaches itself to the wall of the uterus. The female is pregnant, and the united cell can develop into a baby.

Chapter 2
Making Decisions

Holly followed the nurse into a cramped office. A small sign reading "Sonia Jackson MSW" occupied the corner of a large wooden desk. Facing the desk sat two rather shabby looking chairs.

Entering the office, Holly slumped into a chair that was comfortable if a little threadbare. "Ms. Jackson will be with you in just a few minutes," said the nurse. "Good luck to you."

Thankful for a spot to sit and gather her thoughts, Holly looked around the office. Small plastic holders full of all kinds of literature covered a side table. Posters plastered the walls, some highlighting the harmful effects of smoking on unborn babies, others warning teens to seek help if they were victims of abuse. A plastic model of the female reproductive system sat on the other end of the desk. Holly observed it with interest until she noted the tiny plastic embryo inside the uterus. For some reason that sight made her feel nauseated all over again.

A short knock sounded on the door, and an attractive middle-aged woman poked her head into the office. "Holly?"

Holly nodded her head.

"Hello, Holly. My name is Sonia Jackson, and I am a social worker employed by this clinic as a counselor. I was told you needed to talk to someone about a pregnancy."

"Uh . . . yeah. I mean, I probably do need to talk to someone. I just found out."

"You just found out you are pregnant? You didn't take any home pregnancy tests?" Ms. Jackson came in, shut the door behind her, and seated herself behind the desk.

"No. I didn't really think I could be—pregnant, that is. But I didn't get my period, and I've been really sick. So I decided to skip class and come down here."

"And so, now you know that you are pregnant. Do you have any plans? Have you made any decisions about whether or not you are going to continue the pregnancy?"

"I don't know, it really hasn't hit me yet, I don't think. Continue the pregnancy? You mean like have an abortion?"

"Well, terminating the pregnancy is one option available to you. Actually, you have a lot of options. It was a good idea for you to come in today, because getting information is the key to making sound decisions. Now you know for sure that you are pregnant, you know that you appear to be in good health, and that you are about two months in to your pregnancy. That is all important information to have. What other information do you need? That's my job, I'm here to tell you about the options that you have available to you. I can help you find out about the different kinds of help that are open to you in our community and put you in touch with people and programs that can assist you."

"You keep talking about options and decisions, but what you are really asking me is if I'm going to have the baby or get rid of it by having an abortion, right?"

"No, not at all. There are a lot of things to consider in your situation, and having an abortion is just one of them. You have mentioned an abortion a few times, though, so why don't we talk about that for a minute. There are two different kinds of abortion procedures. One is a chemical abortion, where you take a combination of drugs to end your pregnancy and cause your body to expel the remains of the pregnancy. This happens at home, and is basically like having a very heavy period. However, this procedure is usually only available to women who are less than eight weeks pregnant, and our exam today shows you to be a little farther along than that. The other type of abortion is more common, and in that procedure a doctor dilates your cervix and empties your uterus, either by scraping or suction, ending the pregnancy. We can refer you to a local doctor who performs this procedure, and it costs about $500. If you want some medication for pain during the procedure that can cost a little extra, but the whole thing only takes about ten minutes."

"Would I have to be in the hospital or miss school?"

"No, the entire process takes place in the doctor's office. You would have cramping and discomfort for probably about one day after the abortion and bleeding that could last for up to two weeks."

"And if I did that no one would have to know, right?"

"Well, your medical records are confidential. So no one would know unless you choose to tell them. But, Holly, this is a very important and tough decision to make. Aren't there any people in your life that you would like to share this with? Maybe people who you trust to help you make a good choice?"

Holly bit her lip. "I've been thinking a lot about my mom today, but I think she would totally lose it if she even knew that Scott and I had sex, let alone me getting pregnant."

"Are you and your mother close?"

"Most of the time we are. But she doesn't really like my boyfriend that much. It has kind of been a problem lately."

"What about your boyfriend? His name is Scott, right? What do you think he would think about this?"

"I don't know. At first it was all 'I love you' and 'We'll always have each other,' but since I started worrying about being pregnant, he's been kinda avoiding me. He even sort of yelled at me yesterday when I asked him to come here with me. He said there was no way he could have gotten me pregnant since he pulled out when we were doing it, you know. Almost like he was saying if I was pregnant it wasn't his problem."

"I'm sure that was very hurtful to you, Holly. And unfortunately, you may be right. Statistically many teen fathers do not visit or support their children. Scott may not think that this pregnancy is his problem, and that may mean that if you decide to choose parenting as an option, you would be doing so without his help. Can you tell me more about your relationship?"

Holly explained that she didn't think Scott would want to be involved in parenting a child.

"Can't I make him pay me child support or something?"

Ms. Jackson smiled at Holly. "Yes, you can go after him for child support. But raising a baby on your own is a huge responsibility and a lot of work, whether you get a support check each month or not. Have you considered the possibility of putting your baby up for adoption?"

Holly shrugged. "Not really. I mean, I haven't given much thought to any of it yet. This all just happened today and, it's . . . I just. . ." Holly began to sob into her hands. Ms. Jackson came out from behind the desk, picked up a box of Kleenex, and handed several to Holly. Holly picked up her head and began to wipe at her eyes.

Ms. Jackson put her hand on Holly's shoulder. "Whatever happens I'm here to help you, okay?"

Holly gulped back her tears. "I know, thanks for spending your time with me. I still can't really believe this is happening. And the thing is, I always planned on being a mom and having a cute baby to dress up and play with, but I thought I would be older and married and stuff, you know?" Holly sniffled and continued to dab at her eyes. "The longer I sit here, the more real it starts to seem. All I can think about is that I don't really want to get an abortion, but at the same time I don't want to have to quit school, and have to tell my parents and my friends. I don't have a job, I don't have any money to buy diapers or pay a doctor. On the other hand, I don't think I could carry a baby for nine months and then hand it over to complete strangers and go back to my life. And if I have this baby, I'm pretty sure Scott is gonna dump me. The whole thing is completely hopeless!"

Ms. Jackson put her hand on Holly's arm. "One thing I can tell you for sure—nothing is hopeless. Look, if you decide to continue the pregnancy, there are a lot of different agencies in our community designed to help you. We have a crisis pregnancy center that will help get you started with all of your baby equipment. They have parenting classes where you can learn how to take care of your baby and meet other girls your age who are going through the same thing. The school district offers a special program for teen parents so that you can still finish high school. If you don't have medical coverage, Medicaid is a federal program that will pay your medical expenses during your pregnancy and pay for medical care for the baby after its born. Legal Aid can help you in getting your baby's father to pay support. If you don't have a place to stay once you have your baby, one of our local Catholic churches runs a shelter for young mothers. Whatever your decision is, there is a support system here in our community to help you cope."

Holly sat up straighter in her chair and wiped the last of her tears off her face. "Do you really think I can do this by myself?"

"That's not a question for me to answer. I guess what I'm telling you is that if you decide you want to keep your baby, you don't have to do it all by yourself. There are people willing to help." Ms. Jackson gave Holly's shoulders a squeeze before returning to her chair on the other side of the desk.

Holly sat looking at her hands in her lap for several minutes before speaking again. "Do you have any brochures or flyers from those places you were telling me about? You know, like the place with the classes, and the school district program, and the Medicaid and legal aid stuff?"

"Of course. Did you want any information about any of the other things we talked about to help you make your decision?"

Holly stood up and tossed her crumpled tissue into the small silver wastebasket. "No. I know what I'm going to do. I just want that stuff so I can try to explain it to my mom and dad."

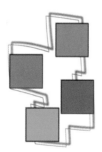

Pregnancy

Pregnancy is the period of time before birth during which a fertilized egg plants itself inside the lining of the uterus, grows inside the uterus, and eventually develops into a baby.

A missed period does not automatically mean a woman is pregnant. At the same time, vaginal bleeding does not always indicate a period. Usually if a menstrual period is one or two days early or late, there is no cause for concern. However, a delay may be a sign of pregnancy. If a woman misses more than two periods in a row or suspects she is pregnant, she

Once it reaches the uterus, the embryo is at the blastocyst stage, when an inner mass of cells, which will become the fetus, forms. The outer mass of cells will become the placenta.

should consult a health-care professional. Sometimes worrying about the possibility of pregnancy can delay a period.

The physical signs of pregnancy are obvious to some women. They may have a sensitivity to certain aromas, such as coffee, grease, or cigarette smoke. Women may experience nausea and vomiting when they wake up. This is often called "morning sickness." Fatigue and a greater desire to sleep are common complaints. Many women have the need to urinate more frequently. They may crave certain foods. Their breasts are enlarged and tender. As the pregnancy progresses, a woman will notice her abdomen getting larger and feel movement in her belly.

To determine if she is pregnant, a woman can purchase a home pregnancy test at most drugstores. These tests are simple to use, but they may be inaccurate. The test will give a reliable answer as early as the first day of a missed period. To be certain if she is pregnant, a woman should have a urine or blood test performed by a health-care professional.

What Next?

An unplanned pregnancy can cause a teen to experience mixed emotions. When she discovers she is pregnant, she may react with fear and disbelief. She may have feelings of guilt and anxiety. Or she may be excited and scared at the same time. She may ask herself: What should I do? Should I have an abortion? Should I tell my parents? Should I tell my boyfriend? What will people think? How will this change the rest of my life?

Choices

Once a young woman has confirmed she is pregnant, she will need to make some difficult decisions. Every choice will impact both the mother and the baby, as well as other people. Sometimes teens know immediately what they will do, while others need time to consider their options. The young woman may want to sort through her feelings before sharing the results with someone. She will probably feel scared. Besides seeing a health-care provider, the young woman should talk honestly with her parents or an adult she trusts and with the baby's father. A man may not be excited when he first hears the news; he

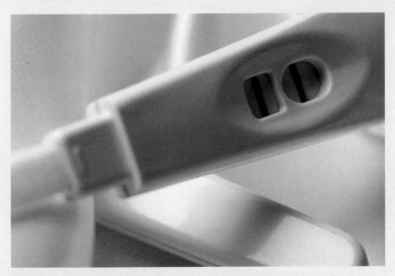

If a woman suspects she is pregnant, she may purchase a home pregnancy test from most drugstores. However, a visit to a health-care professional is the best way to be certain that she is pregnant.

may be worried or afraid. Parents may have similar reactions. An unplanned pregnancy is difficult for everyone concerned.

After carefully considering her options, a woman may decide to have an abortion or terminate the pregnancy. The word abort means to stop or to end something at an early stage. Miscarriage is an abortion that occurs naturally and spontaneously, while an induced abortion is a medical procedure done by choice to interrupt an unwanted pregnancy. A doctor or other trained health-care professional usually performs the procedure in a clinic or hospital. Removing the embryo or fetus from the uterus ends the pregnancy.

The abortion pill called RU 486 is a two-drug chemical abortion. The first drug causes the uterine lining to shed, disconnecting the fetus. A second drug is taken a day or two later and causes the womb to expel the now-dead embryo. Taken one after the other, the two drugs cause an induced abortion.

Some family-planning clinics offer counseling as well as provide abortion services. Abortion may not be an option for some people because of religious or personal beliefs, or because the pregnancy is already too far along. Abortion is a difficult, life-changing decision.

A woman's decision whether or not to terminate the pregnancy must be made early in the pregnancy. If she decides to not terminate, she has to decide if she will choose adoption or raise the child. Some teenage girls are convinced adoption is the best choice, while others cannot bear the idea of giving away the baby.

Adoption

Adoption usually occurs when a parent or parents are unable to take care of their newborn baby. The parent decides to have someone else care for, bring up, and love the baby. Pregnant teens who are not ready to be parents have the option to let someone else raise the child. Many women who choose adoption are happy knowing that their children are loved and living in good homes with adults who are eager to be parents.

The decision to have sex may initially seem exciting. However, choosing not to use condoms can lead to scarier decisions if an unplanned pregnancy occurs.

Adoption is a legal act. The birth parent or parents sign a paper saying they are giving their child forever to parents who want to and are able to take care of the child. The new adoptive parents agree to raise the child as their own. They also sign the adoption paper in front of a lawyer or a judge. Most states require adoptive parents to pass a home study by a licensed agency or professional. Adoption laws are different in every state, and all adoptions must be approved by a judge.

In an *open adoption*, the names of the birth mother (and sometimes of the birth father) and the adoptive parents are known to one another. The birth mother may select the adoptive parents. She and the adoptive parents may exchange letters and photographs. They may also choose to meet, and to have an ongoing relationship. A *closed adoption* keeps the names of the birth mother and the adoptive parents secret from one another.

Thousands of women and men are waiting to adopt newborn children. Many people choose to adopt children because they are not able to conceive a baby. Some people who can conceive a baby also choose to adopt children. If a person is considering adoption, information and confidential advice are available from adoption agencies or social service departments.

Pregnancy changes lives. Giving up a baby for adoption is difficult. Being a single parent is difficult. Being a single teen parent is even more difficult. Even having an abortion cannot totally erase the entire pregnancy as though it had never existed. Choosing to have an abortion has its own set of consequences. When a teenager is pregnant, she needs to talk through all the possible consequences of each of her decisions so that she can be sure she is making the decision that is right for her.

Some teenagers are fortunate enough to be able to live with their parents who will help them through the entire process. Other teens are less fortunate and are forced to find other living conditions. A teenager may receive a lot of advice about her pregnancy. She may even feel pressured into doing something that someone else thinks is right. In the end, the young woman will have to live with her decision the rest of her life.

Chapter 3
Telling Family and Friends

Holly entered the front door of her house that afternoon the same way she did every day after school. She dropped her backpack on a table next to the front door and walked through her parent's four-bedroom home to the kitchen, hoping to find a snack that wouldn't make her puke. As she grabbed a red-gold apple from the basket of fruit on the kitchen counter, Holly now saw the home where she had spent her entire life with new eyes. Looking around at her surroundings, Holly realized how very fortunate she was to have been born into the family she had been. Would her baby ever come home from school to a comfortable place like this—or would she be raising her child in a church shelter or a dingy apartment somewhere?

Sitting in the office with Ms. Jackson, Holly had begun to see herself as a mother to a sweet little baby. It might even be kind of fun. Now that she was back in her own home, though, Holly realized that as she had envisioned herself holding her baby, she had imagined herself sitting in the rocker in her parents' living room. What if that wasn't possible? What if her parents kicked her out? Where would she go?

Holly's fears suddenly seemed more than she could handle. Her parents would be home from work in a couple of hours. Exhausted, too overwhelmed to think any more, Holly climbed the stairs to her room and fell asleep.

In the end, Holly's parents took the news much better than she had ever thought they would. She had decided to tell her mother first, thinking she would let her mom break the news to her dad. However, once her mom had gotten an idea of where their talk was headed, she insisted they call Holly's dad in to join them right away. She said it was a "family matter" and that he shouldn't be left out. Holly knew they were disappointed in her and also pretty angry. But when it came right down to it, they loved her and wanted to do whatever they could to help her.

At first Holly's dad had felt strongly that she should have an abortion. He pointed out to Holly that having a baby now would interfere with just about every plan she had ever made for her life. She had always been a good student and had hoped to attend college to become a veterinarian. Now, her father reminded her, even if Holly could manage to complete her schooling and achieve that goal, it would be extremely difficult. He also asked her to think about the fact that getting that kind of education would probably take her much longer than she had originally planned, and when she did finish, she would have a child who was already in junior high.

Holly's mother had a different set of concerns. "Holly, you know we love you and will support you in whatever choice you make, but I think it's important that you understand what I mean by support. We will help you finish school, we will help you to make sure you have a place to live and food to eat. We will help you to make sure you get access to health care. But what we won't do is raise this baby for you. If you decide to have this baby, you need to know it will be *your* baby. You will be getting up and walking the floor with it every night. You will be feeding it, and bathing it, and changing diapers. You will be finding child care for it while you work and attend school. We love you and we will love your baby, but we won't parent it for you. If you choose to continue with this pregnancy, then you are making a choice to accept this responsibility."

Having a baby suddenly didn't sound like so much fun, now that Holly was imagining waking up every night to take care of it. But the biggest problem came when she and her parents got around to discussing Scott. Holly's mother was furious he hadn't even gone to the clinic with Holly for the pregnancy test. Her dad wanted to call Scott's parents and have them come over to the house; he thought they should explain what they were willing to contribute to help Holly through her pregnancy and find out what kind of role they planned to play after the baby was born.

At last, Holly was able to talk them out of it. Scott didn't even know that she was pregnant yet. She had tried his cell a couple of times after leaving the clinic, but he had never answered the phone. Holly knew she and Scott needed time alone together to work all of this out.

Unfortunately, time alone with Scott was very hard to come by. He wasn't answering her calls, he avoided her at school, and one day she waited for him by his car, only to hear he had gotten a ride home from a friend. Hurt and confused, Holly ended up that afternoon alone in the girls' room at school, crying. Her friend Tina came looking for her and listened patiently as Holly cried on her shoulder.

At first, Holly felt better. Tina was the first person she had told besides her parents, and she was very sympathetic.

But Holly didn't feel better for long. Tina went straight to Scott and told him what a loser she thought he was for not sticking by Holly during such a rough time. So not only did Scott find out for sure that Holly was pregnant from someone else, he found out in front of a group of his friends. His reaction was pretty harsh.

"Whatever!" he shouted at Holly from the other end of the school hallway. "I know it's not mine. If you really are pregnant, you must have been hooking up with someone else." Then he stormed down the stairs without ever coming close enough to Holly that she could have answered him without shouting.

By 3:15 that afternoon, the whole school knew Holly's big secret. Most of them thought that she had gotten pregnant by someone other than Scott.

Scott did eventually catch up with Holly a few days later as she was walking home from school. He pulled his car over and offered her a ride as she walked the short distance from her bus stop to her house. As she got in, Scott looked at her face; maybe he noticed for the first time how bad she looked. Holly knew her eyes showed signs of all the tears she'd been crying recently, and she hadn't slept well for days. She hoped he felt at least a twinge of guilt as he looked at her. When he didn't seem to know what to say, Holly saved him the trouble by speaking first.

"How could you think it wasn't yours?"

"Well, I mean . . . is it?"

"You know it is. You know I haven't been with anyone besides you."

"Well, I didn't think I could get you pregnant, the way that we did it I mean."

"But you did get me pregnant, Scott, and I'm having this baby. So what are we going to do about it?"

His face turned red. "What do you mean—we? You're having it. There's nothing I can do."

"Sure there is." Holly tried to hold on to her temper. "You could get a job and help me pay for all the stuff this baby's going to need. You could tell me you still love me and that we're going to stay together and you're going to help me raise our baby. You could stick around and help me with feedings and change diapers. Are you going to do any of those things?" The car had come to a stop in front of Holly's house.

Scott hung his head. "Holly, I don't think I can. I mean, I never planned on anything like this. I have a lot of things going on right now. I can't tell my parents; you know they'll totally freak out. Plus, I'm really involved in sports right now, and I'm real busy just trying to keep my grades up. I'm headed off to college in August. I have a scholarship and everything. I can't mess that up."

"Well, that's just perfect, Scott." Holly heard her voice soaring higher and higher, but she no longer cared about controlling her temper. "I'd love to see you off when you go to school this summer, but it looks like I'm busy in August. Our baby will be about a month old by then." With that, Holly got out of the car and slammed the door behind her. She ran into the house without once looking back.

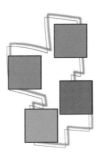

Many teen pregnancies are unexpected and at first unwanted, but some are wanted and even planned. Some young women may try to find pleasure and fulfillment by having babies. They view motherhood as a way to become more grown up and independent. Some teenagers want to escape a difficult home life or want a reason to quit school. Others crave a relationship. These young women want someone to love, someone who will love them unconditionally in return. Often a woman with low self-esteem doesn't think much of herself or her future. She doesn't have

Some girls dream of the day when they will have an adorable baby of their very own. However, teens need to realize there are many financial and personal challenges involved in caring for a baby.

any reason to delay pregnancy. Still others believe pregnancy and children are solutions to boredom, loneliness, or lack of direction. These young women may lack goals, they may not like school, and they may have grown up in poverty. Often they have grown up without fathers. They may think having a child is the best way to keep a boyfriend. Motherhood is viewed as an escape from their difficult circumstances to a more exciting lifestyle. Unfortunately, it rarely turns out that way.

Clearly, a teen who decides to keep her baby will face many challenges. When making her decisions, she needs to consider these carefully. Her individual circumstances will make a difference, so she should ask herself these questions:

- What are my spiritual and moral beliefs?
- Is raising a child by myself the best choice for the child and me?
- Is raising a child with my partner the best choice for the child and me?
- Is placing the baby for adoption the best choice for the baby and me?
- How would each choice affect my everyday life?
- Which choice could I live with?
- Which choice would be impossible for me?
- How much support can I count on from my parents or other family members?
- What kind of support will my family offer (babysitting, financial aid, a place to live)?

- How much support can I count on from the baby's father?

- What kind of support will the father offer (child care, financial aid, help from his family)?

- What programs are available in my area for pregnant teens? (Does my high school offer support? Are there other support agencies in the area? What other organizations will offer me help?)

- How do I cope with physical and emotional stress?

- Do I have good friends who will support me?

- Am I good at handling more than one responsibility at once?

- Am I willing to set aside the time I spend having fun in order to care for a child?

Pregnancy and Adolescent Males

Some men think being able to reproduce proves their manhood and maturity. They may have feared they would not be able to perform sexually. Even though contraceptives usually are easy to obtain, some males don't always use birth control because they think birth control is inconvenient or interferes with sexual pleasure.

A teenage father will probably have opinions about what his girlfriend should do regarding a pregnancy—but in most states he has no legal right as to whether or not the woman terminates the pregnancy. However, this doesn't mean he should be excluded from discussions. His attitude and support will help the woman make her decision.

Fathers have rights once the baby is born, and with those rights come all the responsibilities of having a family. Unfortunately, few teenage fathers help maintain their children. Many teenage fathers don't even see their children. A community program may offer tutoring as well as counseling for teenage fathers. The counselors advise fathers to stay in school or help him find a job if he is ready to work. Job opportunities and hourly wages are often limited for young males, which means it may be difficult for them to offer financial support. The girl's family sometimes offers further barriers to the male staying involved with the child.

It's not easy being a teenage father, either!

Chapter 4
Staying Healthy

This is very good Holly. You've gained four pounds since your last visit."

Holly groaned and rolled her eyes toward the ceiling as the nurse set the weights back to zero on the scale. Holly stepped down and slipped her flip-flops back on her feet. "Same room as last time, Holly. The doctor will be in with the ultrasound machine in just a few minutes."

Holly had been waiting for this visit. She was now twenty weeks along, and the doctors had told her that she could probably learn her baby's sex this time when they looked at it with the ultrasound machine. She had asked Scott if he wanted to come—but she wasn't really surprised when he didn't want to. Instead, her mom was there to catch a glimpse of her first grandchild.

Holly stepped into the exam room while the nurse went to fetch her mother from the waiting room. Everyone was always saying that she hardly looked pregnant, but she felt like a whale. She had started out a little underweight, though, and because teen mothers are more at risk for having low birth-weight babies, Holly's doctors wanted her to gain about thirty to thirty-five pounds during her pregnancy. So far she had gained nine pounds. Everyone but Holly seemed happy with that.

Her mother was seated in a chair next to the examining table when Dr. Ramos came in, pushing the ultrasound machine in front of him. It was basically a computer on a cart with a couple of funny looking wands instead of a mouse. Dr. Ramos greeted them both. He had known Holly's mother for years; he was the one who had delivered Holly when she was a baby, after all. It was comforting to Holly to have her medical care in the hands of someone she trusted.

Dr. Ramos started out by determining how big Holly's uterus had grown. He used a tape measure to measure the number of centimeters from Holly's pubic bone to the fundus, the top of her uterus. The number of centimeters should be roughly equal to the number of weeks Holly was pregnant, and Dr. Ramos announced, "Twenty centimeters." Dr. Ramos did this every visit, since it was an easy way to make sure that the baby was growing properly.

Next, he told Holly the results of her last blood tests. This was a part of the exam that Holly was not prepared for early in her pregnancy, since she had always been very afraid of needles. By now, she was getting used to it. Initially, they had tested her for sexually transmitted diseases. Then she had tests for certain blood markers that could tell if her baby was likely to have some kinds of birth defects like Down syndrome or spina bifida. Fortunately, those tests had all come back just fine. The last test had been to test for gestational diabetes. She had to have blood drawn, drink an awful-tasting syrup, and then wait an hour and have more blood drawn. Again, Dr. Ramos said that test had been completely normal as well.

There were other tests that happened at every visit. The nurses kept a very close watch on Holly's weight and blood pressure. Any dramatic changes in either could indicate a dangerous health problem. They tested Holly's urine each visit as well, checking for dangerous sugar levels, which could indicate diabetes; protein, which might mean kidney problems; or bacteria, which could signify an infection. All these tests had always been perfectly normal each month as well.

Holly had begun to feel the baby move a couple of weeks ago, and so now there was another way to assess the baby's well-being. Holly liked feeling her baby move inside her, because she knew that meant the baby was healthy and strong. Dr. Ramos had told her to call him if she didn't feel the baby move for more than twenty-four hours, but somehow Holly didn't think that would be a problem. In fact, she wouldn't be surprised if this baby turned out to be a gymnast; it was starting to keep her up at night moving!

Holly's nausea and vomiting had tapered off after her third month, the period when "morning sickness" traditionally comes to an end. The breast tenderness, which had been almost unbearable in the beginning, had started to ease as well. Now, though, she had a few new sources of discomfort.

For instance, every now and then she would get a shooting pain on the side of her abdomen. At first she had been alarmed, but the doctor had assured her that these pains were normal. Called "round ligament pains," they were caused by the pressure her growing uterus was putting on the ligaments in her sides. Sometimes she got shooting pains down the back of her legs too, called sciatica, from the pressure of her uterus on an important nerve. The doctor had recommended cutting back on the number of books Holly carried in her backpack as a way to help avoid those pains. And her growing belly was putting more pressure on her stomach, causing a lot of heartburn, so Holly carried Tums with her everywhere now and ate them the way she used to eat candy. But still, all things considered, she was feeling pretty good and her pregnancy was going well.

Holly was feeling better emotionally as well. She had gone to the Crisis Pregnancy Center like Ms. Jackson had recommended, and she was now taking a parenting class with some other girls her age there. The Pregnancy Center also offered counseling services that were helping Holly cope with the emotional issues of having to move so quickly from the role of a child into the role of a parent. The counselor had been useful in helping her to deal with all of the hurt and frustration surrounding her relationship with Scott as well.

Shortly after the talk Holly had with Scott that day in the car, Holly's parents had contacted Scott's parents. Scott had not told them about the baby, but their response was similar to his. They didn't feel obligated to do anything for Holly until the baby was born and a paternity test proved that Scott was the father. Even then, Scott's mother pointed out that since Scott would be attending college in the summer, Holly would be awarded limited child support based on the fact that he would be a full-time student. Scott's parents felt that Holly should have had an abortion, since that was what Scott wanted her to do; in their opinion, she had chosen to have the baby by herself, and she needed to live with the consequences—without involving their son.

Scott himself wavered between ignoring the situation and offering Holly limited bits of help. Half the time he ignored her phone calls, but then one day, he called out of the blue and asked to go with her to the doctor. He laughed and held her hand as they listened together to their baby's heartbeat. Holly had been filled with hope—but a few days later, he went back to ignoring her phone calls. She and Scott had discussed the possibility of him attending a childbirth preparation class with Holly and being there to support her during the birth, but Holly knew better now than to depend on Scott. Her mom would attend the classes with her, just like it was her mom sitting next to her today.

Dr. Ramos squirted a blob of blue gel onto Holly's belly. He told her that the gel would help to conduct the sound waves that the ultrasound machine used to get a picture of the baby. Soon Holly was looking at a grainy black and white image of her child. The baby must have known it was picture day, because it delighted its mother and grandmother, first by grabbing onto its feet and another time by sucking its thumb. After giving Holly a few minutes to watch the baby's profile, the doctor turned to the serious medical examinations for which the ultrasound was designed.

Dr. Ramos photographed the baby's beating heart, making sure it was the appropriate size for the baby's gestational age and checking for four separate chambers. He got pictures of the lungs, which were practicing for breathing by inhaling and exhaling amniotic fluid. He checked the baby's spine for neural tube defects and measured the baby's head circumference. This reassured them that the baby's brain was growing properly. They looked at the baby's kidneys and stomach, made sure there were two hands and two feet with five fingers or toes on each. A measurement was taken of the baby's femur. This helped to make sure that Holly's due date was correct, since it is a good indication of how long the baby had been growing.

Finally, Dr. Ramos asked if Holly wanted to know her baby's gender. Holly nodded. Dr. Ramos slid the ultrasound probe down Holly's belly, giving her another view of her baby's legs. When the baby suddenly turned on its own, Holly gasped; even on the grainy screen the baby's sex was obvious to her.

"Congratulations, Holly," said Dr. Ramos. "It's a boy!"

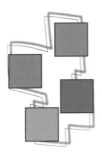

Prenatal Care

If a woman decides to not terminate the pregnancy, she should begin *prenatal* care as soon as possible— whether she considers adoption or decides to raise the child herself. A medical exam early in the pregnancy will help make sure she is healthy and the pregnancy is normal. A healthy pregnancy requires a certain lifestyle. She should not smoke, not drink alcohol, and not use drugs. While the woman is deciding what to do after the baby is born, she needs to take good care of herself and the developing baby.

Gestation

Gestation is the time between conception and the birth of the baby, when the baby is growing inside the mother's womb. In human beings, pregnancy or gestation averages 266 days or forty weeks from conception. This is 280 days or about nine months from the beginning of the last menstrual period. The gestation period is divided into three trimesters. Each trimester is three months.

The baby grows in the uterus—not in the stomach. By attaching to the wall of the uterus, the developing baby is able to receive nutrition from the mother's glands and blood vessels within the uterine lining. In the uterus, a sac filled with a watery fluid forms around the developing baby and protects it against pokes, bumps, and jolts. The sac is called the amniotic sac or the "bag of waters," and the fluid is called amniotic fluid. This fluid is warm and keeps the developing baby warm as it floats. As the developing baby grows bigger, the uterus grows bigger. Early in pregnancy, a structure forms in the uterus that enables the embryo to receive the food, water, and oxygen it needs. This is called the placenta.

The umbilical cord is a rope-like cord that connects the placenta to the fetus. The placenta supplies the fetus with oxygen from the air the mother breathes and nutrients from the food she eats. Oxygen and nutrients pass from the placenta to the fetus in the blood that flows through the umbilical cord. Waste from the fetus leaves the mother's body along with the mother's waste.

Medicines, drugs, and alcohol can also pass into the developing baby's blood from the mother's

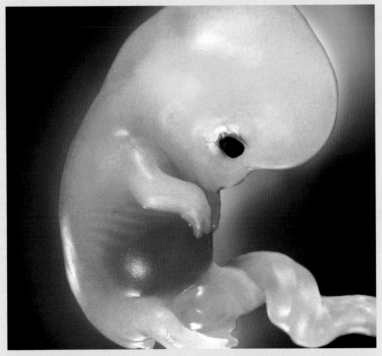

In its earliest stages, a human embryo does not resemble a baby as we know it. However, after about 8 weeks, arms and legs are recognizable and the developing baby is called a fetus.

blood. That's why a pregnant female should be very careful about what she eats, drinks, and puts into her body. If she needs to take a drug—prescription or over-the-counter—she should check with her health-care provider to make sure the drug will not hurt the fetus.

If a female has smoked cigarettes, consumed alcohol, taken drugs, or had certain infections while pregnant, her baby could be born with or develop serious health problems. The baby could have difficulty eating, breathing, and growing properly. If a pregnant woman has been addicted to drugs, her baby may be born addicted to drugs. However, if the woman has regular checkups with a health-care provider, eats healthy foods, exercises regularly,

When she is pregnant, everything a woman eats, drinks or inhales also passes along to the baby. Therefore, alcohol and cigarette use should be discontinued and a woman should consult her doctor before taking even over-the-counter medicines.

and gets enough sleep, her baby will have the best chance to be born healthy.

Healthy Hints for Pregnancy

- Eat good foods (fruits, vegetables, cereals, breads, beans, rice, dairy products, fish, meat, and poultry).
- Drink eight glasses of water every day.
- Stay active and get regular exercise.
- Get plenty of sleep.
- Do not eat junk food.
- Do not drink alcohol or drinks with caffeine, such as coffee or soda.
- Do not smoke.
- Do not take any drugs or medications—even aspirin—without checking with your health-care provider.

Going to the Doctor

A pregnant woman's first prenatal visit will include a complete physical exam and reviewing her medical history. The health-care provider will check the woman's vital signs and listen to her heart and lungs. The woman needs to get used to being weighed because it happens at each appointment during a pregnancy. A mother's weight is one tool to help determine if the baby is developing. The woman should gain approximately two pounds a month (depending in part on her pre-pregnancy weight). The health-care provider will also determine the woman's due date if it has not yet been decided.

A gynecological exam is also called a pelvic exam, vaginal exam, or internal exam. During this exam, the woman lies on her back on the examining table. She places her feet in metal footrests and is asked to keep her knees apart. The health-care provider checks the external genital organs for any sores or lesions that might indicate a sexually transmitted disease, such as herpes. Then using a **speculum**, the health-care provider views the cervix. Also, the health-care provider gently examines the size and position of the uterus, the fallopian tubes, and the ovaries, with one hand on top of the woman's abdomen and index and middle fingers in the vagina. The health-care provider may perform a rectal exam, feeling inside the anus and rectum for lumps, swelling or obstruction. This exam includes checking a woman's breasts for lumps.

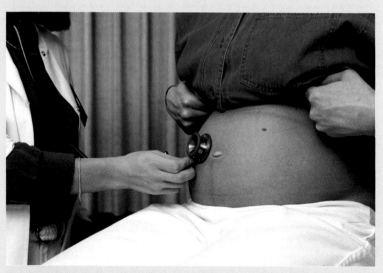

Once a woman decides to keep her baby, she should begin prenatal care as soon as possible. Her doctor will monitor both her health and the baby's health.

The health-care provider should explain everything that takes place during the exam. However, many women are nervous during a gynecological exam. To relax, a woman can take slow, deep breaths. Talking, asking questions, or sharing concerns with the health-care provider during the exam may also help ease emotional tension.

At the earliest time that it's possible to determine a pregnancy exists, the embryo will already be four or six weeks' gestation. If there are no problems, the pregnant teen should be able to continue attending school. She will be tired because her body is producing more blood. She may also feel nauseated or sick to her stomach. Some women are sick every morning. Eating a few saltine crackers before getting out of bed in the morning will help. The woman may have to urinate frequently. During this first trimester, the pregnant teen's breasts may feel tender and heavy as milk glands begin to grow.

The First Trimester

The first trimester is the first twelve weeks of pregnancy. During this trimester, a pregnant woman's body changes significantly. A sperm joins an ovum to form one cell during Week One. This **zygote** is smaller than a grain of salt. Once this happens, the developing human is called an embryo. During Week Two, the fertilized egg implants itself in the lining of the uterus and begins to take nourishment. A woman is still unaware of her pregnancy during Week Three, but she is about to miss her first menstrual period. At one month old (Week Four), the embryo is ten thousand times larger than the original fertilized egg.

The backbone and muscles are forming. Arms, legs, eyes, and ears have begun to show.

During Week Five, the developing baby's leg and arm buds are now clearly visible. Week Six is when the mother is about to miss her second period and has probably confirmed she is pregnant. The brain begins to control movement of muscles and organs. At Week Seven, the embryo begins to move spontaneously. Tooth buds form in the gums.

Week Eight is when the developing baby is called a fetus. Although the mother will not be able to feel movement until the fourth or fifth month, the fetus responds to touch. Fingerprints are evidenced in the skin during Week Nine, and internal organs are present and functioning. Changes after this week are primarily changes in size, rather than in appearance. The uterus has doubled in size at Week Ten. The fetus can squint, swallow, and wrinkle its forehead. At Week Eleven, the fetus is about two inches long, and the face has a baby's profile. The fetus sleeps, awakens, and exercises its muscles at Week Twelve. The first trimester closes at the end of the third month.

The Second Trimester

For many women, the second trimester is the most comfortable time of pregnancy. Women at this stage of pregnancy often feel better and are not concerned yet about the third-trimester delivery. During this trimester, the woman's uterus grows significantly as the baby undergoes a tremendous growth spurt. Not only does the woman's outward appearance change, her body continues making internal changes, too. She may not feel sick to her stomach, and food will even start to smell good again. The woman will have increased energy. As a result of the presence or increase in hormones, her hair may become thicker and more luxurious than usual. The extra hair growth is temporary and most will disappear after birth.

However, this stage of pregnancy also has its discomforts. A woman's growing uterus creates upward pressure on her organs. The uterus is entirely separate from the stomach. As the uterus expands, it presses on the bladder and stomach and all the other organs. This explains why the mother needs to urinate more often than usual, and she needs to eat smaller, more frequent meals. Her body needs extra fluid, so she should drink approximately eight to ten

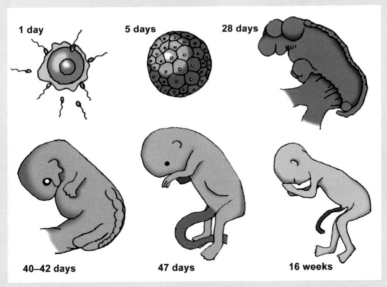

Over the forty weeks of pregnancy, the growing fetus goes through many changes. The mother will also experience dramatic changes to her body as she travels through each of the trimesters of the pregnancy.

Regular exercise is an important part of a healthy pregnancy. However, a woman must always check with her doctor concerning the types and amount of exercise that are safe for her and the baby.

cups a day. The pressure of her growing uterus on her bowels may interfere with elimination and increase the likelihood of constipation. She should take in lots of fluid and fiber in her diet, and moderately exercise if permitted by her health-care provider. She may also experience heartburn and indigestion.

Backaches may become worse as the size of her belly increases and her center of gravity shifts forward. She should not wear high heels. Some women develop varicose veins. A woman can prevent or minimize varicose veins by avoiding pressure on the veins by walking twenty minutes every day to exercise and improve circulation and muscle tone in her legs. Muscle cramps often occur at night. She can ask her health-care provider about taking calcium and potassium supplements.

Dizziness is often caused by a sudden change in position. To prevent dizziness, she should move her legs when sitting, stand up gradually, and put one hand on something for support if she feels light-headed. She may also have more headaches. If she experiences severe headaches and cannot find relief, she should call her health-care provider. She should always consult her health-care provider before taking any medications. Stretch marks occur when the skin is stretched beyond its capacity and tears. When the skin covering a pregnant woman's abdomen is stretched, the skin can become itchy. Frequent massages with moisturizing cream will help decrease itchiness.

She will see her health-care provider approximately every four weeks during the second trimester. In addition to checking the woman's vital signs and weight, the health-care provider will also measure the size of the uterus and listen to the fetal heartbeat. The woman may have additional tests ordered. She should discuss with her health-care provider any concerns she has about changes or discomforts.

At the beginning of the second trimester, the baby is completely formed. At four months its bones have begun to develop, and its arms and legs can move. The mother may now experience *quickening*. One way of describing the first kicks is a feeling like little bubbles or a fluttering in the stomach. Feeling the baby move for the first time makes the pregnancy concrete for many women and their partners. Like many expectant mothers, she may begin to talk to the baby and maybe use a nickname for the baby. At five months, the fetus is about ten inches long if its legs were stretched out straight, and it weighs about three-quarters of a pound. At six months, the fetus is beginning to look a lot like a human baby now, except it is thin and has not yet begun to store up fat. At the end of the second trimester, the baby will be able to move its limbs, make a fist, suck its thumb, and even hiccup.

The Third Trimester

The third trimester is a time for excitement and anxiety. Now the woman feels the baby kicking. Sometimes she can even make out the shape of her baby's foot or rear end pressing against the skin of her abdomen. The mother's emotions will run high. She will become more nervous as the due date gets closer. Fear of the birth process, worries about new responsibilities and finances are added stress for the mother (and father if he is involved). The woman should try to enjoy this time. Often, women play music for the baby. Some women even talk or sing to their unborn babies.

Although the woman is pleased to know the baby will soon be here, the final three months are physically less comfortable for her. The baby grows rapidly and becomes heavier. As her body's center of gravity changes, she is more likely to have accidents on stairs and uneven ground, like gravel or broken sidewalks. Her thirst will increase. The mother's hands, ankles, and feet may swell. She may have to buy larger shoes. She should consider taking off her rings before swelling reaches the point where she cannot remove them. She should elevate her feet

Though the woman will first feel movement during the second trimester, it is during the third trimester that the baby will begin to kick. This is also when the woman's feelings about the pregnancy may be most confused, with excitement about the approaching birth mixed with fear of labor pain and her new responsibilities.

for about an hour each day, avoid sitting for lengthy periods of time, and move around so that circulation increases.

Because the uterus presses down on her bladder, pregnancy **incontinence** may occur when a woman coughs, sneezes, or laughs. To avoid leaking, the woman needs to keep her bladder as empty as possible by urinating frequently. She can also wear a panty liner or a sanitary pad, and be sure to change it frequently. A pregnant woman may develop hemorrhoids. These are varicose or swollen rectal veins that are either internal or bulge out of the anus. They are common when a pregnant woman is constipated and strains to eliminate hard stool. Hemorrhoids may itch and become irritated. They may also bleed, especially after a bowel movement. She can apply ice compresses or ask her health-care provider to recommend a medicated ointment or pad that will help soothe the area. In addition to moderate exercise, drinking lots of fluids, and increasing the fiber content of her diet, the woman's health-care provider can also suggest a stool softener or a fiber supplement.

A woman's heart needs to work harder to improve circulation through the uterus and the placenta. She may begin to feel short of breath. If this happens, she should slow down or take a break if she is in the middle of an activity. Regular exercise improves the efficiency of her respiratory system, circulation, and muscle tone; but she should continue exercising at a slower pace. Changing her position will help. If it is harder to breathe when lying down, she can prop herself with pillows or sleep in a reclining chair. Some women experience more dreams during pregnancy, while others find it difficult to get a good night's sleep. Napping during the day may help.

Pregnant women experience gentle contractions called Braxton-Hicks contractions. These usually last less than one minute and are painless. She will feel as if her uterus is gradually becoming tight and then relaxing. These contractions may be called false labor because they don't lead to childbirth, but sometimes an expectant mother thinks she is about to give birth. She can consider these as practice contractions that help her uterus prepare for the actual delivery.

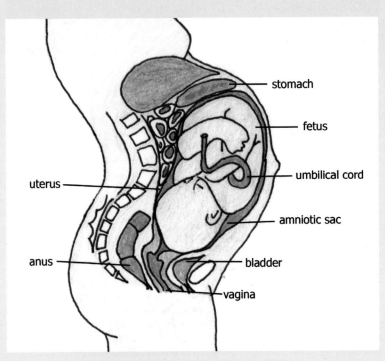

At the end of the third trimester, the baby's size increases rapidly. As a result, the uterus crowds other organs, such as her bladder, causing the need to urinate frequently.

Visits to her health-care provider will be scheduled every other week during the last trimester. Then in the last month, she will see her health-care provider each week until she gives birth. In the ninth month of pregnancy, a woman may stop gaining weight or

Teens are twice as likely to give birth to a premature baby. Preemies born as early as 24 weeks have a chance at survival, but only with proper treatment in the intensive care nursery.

even lose weight. A few weeks before going into labor, some women feel energetic and elated. Routine procedures will be the same as in the second trimester. Also, she will be checked for diabetes. If a woman has diabetes, she will be placed on a low-sugar diet and will be tested regularly for blood-sugar level. The pregnancy should be closely monitored, especially as the due date approaches.

If a woman ever notices a sudden decrease in her baby's movement or if the baby doesn't move at all, the mother should call her health-care provider. This doesn't necessarily mean there are problems, but tests will be taken to assess the baby's well-being. Although problems still occur, the health-care provider can remedy most of them so the mother and baby come through the delivery fine. Encountering a problem during pregnancy or childbirth is always emotionally difficult.

Each day during the third trimester, the baby will gain strength. At seven months it is fourteen inches long and probably weighs over two pounds. The baby is considered viable by the twenty-fourth week and later. This means if the baby is born this early, the baby could survive, with proper medical attention in an intensive-care nursery. Such a baby is called premature, since it is born before the full term of nine months. A premature baby may be born with several problems. Neonatal intensive care units and the use of drugs before and after delivery help more babies survive premature delivery.

During months eight and nine the fetus grows to an average weight of seven or eight pounds. By the beginning of the ninth month, the baby will have long nails on its toes and fingers. At the end of the forty weeks, the baby is ready to be born.

To avoid heartburn and indigestion:

- Eat several small meals throughout the day instead of three big meals.

- Eat slowly, chewing food carefully and completely.

- Eat boiled or broiled food. Do not eat fried, spicy, or fatty foods.

- Do not drink coffee, soda, or alcohol.

- Avoid clothing that puts pressure on the stomach (tight waistbands or belts).

To relieve headache pain, place an ice pack at the back of the mother's neck or on top of her head. Also, fresh air, an hour or two in a quiet dark room, or a nap may lessen the pain.

Smoking and Pregnancy

When the mother smokes, the heartbeat of the fetus speeds up. Mothers who smoke cigarettes tend to have smaller babies and more complications than mothers who do not smoke.

Fetal Alcohol Syndrome

If the mother drinks alcohol, the baby's movements inside the uterus slow down while the alcohol is in the mother's bloodstream. Some babies of mothers who used alcohol during pregnancy are born with a disorder called fetal alcohol syndrome (FAS). This disorder is the third leading cause of birth defects and the number-one cause of mental retardation in the United States. It causes physical deformities and mental retardation. Alcohol use by a pregnant woman is very harmful to the baby, both at birth and through its life.

Drugs and Pregnancy

Drugs are harmful to the baby, especially heroin. As the mother becomes addicted to heroin, the baby also becomes addicted. After the baby is born, the baby goes through painful and serious withdrawal symptoms, just as an adult does when taken off the drug.

Why use an ultrasound?

- to check the fetus
- to verify the due date
- to measure different parts of the fetus
- to verify the location of the placenta
- to check for twins or triplets
- to evaluate the amount of amniotic fluid

The technician and health-care provider may be able to tell if the baby is a boy or a girl. However, sometimes the baby's legs may block the view. If a woman wants to know her baby's gender, she should ask the technician. Some people prefer the surprise of not finding out until the baby is born.

Chapter 5
Labor and Delivery

Holly was hot and uncomfortable. By the end of July, the whole town was suffering from the effects of a heat wave. At 101 degrees, with little breeze and high humidity, everyone was sweltering, especially Holly who was a week past her due date.

Most of the time Holly spent her days indoors, seeking refuge in the air-conditioning. The cool air was a small comfort, however. Her entire body seemed to ache. The skin on her stomach and breasts had stretched so much that she was itchy all the time; no amount of lotion seemed to help. Her back ached constantly, her feet hurt if she stood or walked for any length of time, and the baby's movements were so strong now that he hurt her sometimes.

Holly was also going stir-crazy alone in the house all day long. It was too hot to do much, yet everyone else seemed busy. Since school had ended, she hadn't seen much of her friends. While she was still going to classes, things had seemed almost normal between Holly and her girlfriends. Now she was waddling around in maternity clothes, looking for a bathroom every five minutes while her friends enjoyed their summer vacations in bikinis and sundresses. No one had any time to sit inside with a depressed and uncomfortable pregnant girl.

Scott had stopped by once since school ended, making Holly feel slightly more cheerful. That cheerfulness was short lived though. About two weeks later, she had seen him again while she was shopping for baby clothes at the mall. He was holding hands with a pretty red-haired girl and didn't seem to be worrying a bit that his son would be born any day now. He walked right by her and didn't say a word, although he had been so involved with his new companion it was possible he hadn't actually seen Holly.

Meanwhile, every now and then a contraction would remind Holly that her labor was close at hand, and apprehension would set in. Despite all her childbirth teacher had said about birth being a natural part of life, Holly wasn't sold. There was just no way around the fact that it was going to hurt. A lot, she figured, most likely more than anything else she had ever had to go through. And while she had faithfully practiced her breathing, Holly was pretty sure that when the time came, she would be asking the doctors for drugs.

The contractions Holly had been having so far weren't that bad, though. Dr. Ramos said they were just "Braxton-Hicks" contractions, practice contractions to help get her body ready for the real thing. Usually, they didn't hurt at all, but every now and then one would come on so strong it would take her breath away. Mostly they were annoying because she had to spend so much time trying to decide if they were "real" contractions or not. How long were they lasting, how intense were they, how far apart? Holly didn't think it should be so hard for a doctor to tell you if you were in labor or not.

Holly was going back to see Dr. Ramos again today. Since her due date had passed, she had been seeing him every other day. Because she was so young, and because her blood pressure had gone up a little bit, they were giving her "non-stress tests" to make sure the baby was still healthy. Dr. Ramos was also checking her cervix at every visit to see if she was dilated. Apparently the goal was for her cervix to open up ten centimeters. Last visit she had been at two centimeters. Holly had been excited, thinking that the baby was finally on his way, but the nurse told her she needed to get to three centimeters and have regular contractions before she was officially in labor. As much as Holly was dreading labor, she also couldn't wait to be done with being pregnant.

And at this doctor's visit, Holly got more encouraging news. Her contractions had picked up a little bit as her mom was driving her to Dr. Ramos's office. They continued as she sat in the waiting room, and by the time she got back into the exam room, the doctor was sure she was in labor. He told her there was no rush, but to take her bags and head over to the labor and delivery unit at the hospital. His nurse would call ahead, so they would have a room waiting for her.

Holly's mother was very nervous driving back to the house for Holly's things. She told Holly to wait in the car while she went in to get the bags that for weeks had been packed and waiting for this day. Holly used her mother's absence as an opportunity to call Scott. He didn't answer the phone, as she had suspected he wouldn't, but she left a message on his voice mail that she was in labor and headed to the hospital—just in case he changed his mind and wanted to be there. Holly knew her mother would be upset to see Scott there, but Holly just didn't feel right not letting him know that their son was on his way.

Holly's mom returned quickly with the bags, and they made it to the hospital in about ten minutes. When Holly got there, the nurses had a room waiting for her. It was the same kind of birthing suite she had visited during her childbirth class. Bigger than the usual hospital room, the birthing suite had a special bed with a bottom portion that came off when it was time for delivery. The room also had a big television and a large, cushiony recliner for the support person. The wallpaper was a pale peach with a pretty floral border. Through a doorway, Holly saw an adjoining bathroom with an oversized bathtub. She peeked her head in the doorway and saw that the tub had jets. Holly gave a nervous giggle; these rooms were nicer than a lot of the hotel rooms she had been in.

The nurse took Holly's blood pressure and temperature and helped her change into a gown. She told Holly that they wanted to put her on a monitor for a little while, just to see how the baby was reacting to the contractions; then if everything looked normal, they would take her off the monitor and let her move around. To be attached to the monitor, Holly was asked to get into bed, although she could sit up and watch TV. Two elastic bands with plastic discs on them were placed around her belly. The nurse squirted some of that same gel under the discs that Dr. Ramos had used for the ultrasound. When the nurse turned on the machine, Holly could hear her baby's heartbeat, nice and strong.

Just then another contraction hit, stronger than any of the previous ones. Holly needed a few minutes before she could concentrate on what the nurse was telling her.

"There will be a strip of paper printing out of this machine next to your bed, Holly," said the nurse. "The top line of printing is your baby's heartbeat, see—" She pointed to a series of tiny peaks printed on the monitor strip. "The peaks on the bottom line are your contractions. This lets us see how strong your contractions are, how regular, and how far apart. This also prints for me out at the nurse's station, so even though I'm not here, I can check and see how you and the baby are doing. Depending on how fast you progress, a nurse may be in shortly to start an IV. That way we already have a way to get medicine into your system in an emergency—and we won't have to stop to stick you and get a line in you when you are really uncomfortable from labor. Okay?"

Holly nodded that she understood and lay back on the bed to close her eyes. Her mother told her to try to sleep; she would need her rest for the work of pushing her baby out into the world. Holly thought she was too nervous to sleep, but soon, she dozed off to the sound of her son's heartbeat on the monitor, while her mother sat in the recliner reading a book.

Things were not peaceful for long. The nurses woke Holly up trying to adjust the bands that went to the monitor. "What's wrong?" she asked them.

"No need to worry just yet. We're having a little trouble reading the baby's heartbeat. His heart rate seems to slow down with each contraction and that's not good. But sometimes we get readings like this just because the monitor isn't in a good spot to pick up the baby's heartbeat. We're going to try moving it around. And we're going to get that IV started now too."

Moving the monitor bands around didn't help. A minute or two after the nurse got her IV in place, Dr. Ramos appeared and stood at the edge of the bed. "Holly, it looks like your baby is not handling the stress of labor well. These decelerations we're seeing in his heart rate are dangerous. We're going to have to deliver your baby by cesarean section. You will be moved to a surgical suite down the hall, and we'll give you some medicine to put you to sleep. Your baby will be born through an incision in your abdomen. Would you like your mother to stay with you?"

Tears ran down Holly's cheeks, and she started to shake all over. Her mother sat on the bed and put her arms around Holly. "Of course I'll stay with her." She wiped the tears off her daughter's face and added. "They need to hurry, Holly. But don't worry—it's going to be okay."

Holly was quickly placed on a stretcher and wheeled down the hall. Her mother followed her, now wearing paper surgical scrubs. Once they entered the operating room, a motherly looking doctor with gray hair was at her side almost instantly. "Hi, Holly, I'm Dr. Starr. I'm an anesthesiologist and I'm going to put some medicine in your IV to put you to sleep. When you wake up I'll give you some medicine to help with the pain from the surgery, okay?"

Holly tried to answer her, but her eyes were already growing heavy. Her mother's voice came from somewhere behind her, saying, "Don't worry, I'm here, Holly." Holly saw Dr. Ramos sponge an orange liquid across her belly just before the room went dark.

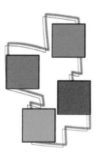

Labor

Chances are labor will not begin on a woman's actual due date. Contractions may begin as twinges that won't interrupt what a woman is doing and eventually reach a point where she can no longer talk through them. A woman's labor may begin with mild contractions that slowly build up over hours, or it may begin with regular and intense contractions. For some women, labor begins after the water has broken.

Labor can be as short as an hour or longer than a day. Labor goes through three stages. During the first stage, contractions cause the cervix to efface (thin) or dilate (open). When the cervix is fully dilated to about ten centimeters, a woman is ready to push. The second stage begins at this point and ends when the baby is born. The length of this stage depends on many factors, including the size of the baby or if the mother has had previous vaginal deliveries. The second stage is when women do their most work. The third stage lasts from the moment the baby is born until the placenta is separated from the wall of the uterus and expelled from the vagina.

A woman's cervix can be fully effaced and a couple of centimeters dilated for a few days or even a couple weeks before she goes into labor. Several other signs indicate when a woman's body is getting ready to go into labor. Engagement refers to the baby's descent into the pelvis. It is also called dropping or lightening. As the baby descends, the mother will find it easier to breathe because the baby is no longer pressing against her diaphragm and lungs. But because the baby is lower, the mother will feel increased pressure on her bowel and bladder, causing constipation and frequent urination. Amniotic fluid should look similar to urine—clear or light yellow. Sometimes it is lightly tinged with blood. A pink-colored or blood-streaked vaginal discharge may appear. This is called the "mucus plug," which usually seals the cervix and becomes loose when the cervix dilates.

Throughout labor, the mother's vital signs will be checked regularly, as well as the dilation of her cervix. If the mother's health-care provider is not already at the hospital, the staff will take the mother's vital signs, listen to the fetal heartbeat, and examine the mother to decide whether or not she should be admitted. The

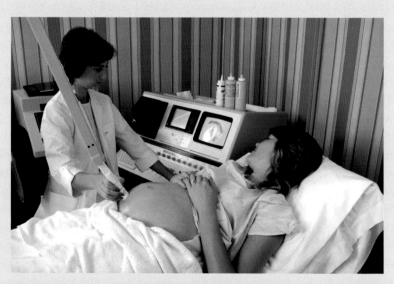

During the first stage of labor, when contractions are causing the cervix to dilate, the woman should go to the hospital. Once she is admitted, a woman's vitals will be monitored until she is ready to begin pushing.

mother may have an intravenous line started. This will give her health-care provider immediate access to the mother's system in case medication is needed.

Pain has always been associated with childbirth. Mothers can now choose to practice natural pain relief techniques or accept medication. The techniques learned in childbirth classes—breathing, focus exercises, and massages—help reduce the pain of childbirth for many women. Narcotics are sometimes used for pain relief in labor. Usually these drugs are injected either through an intravenous line or in the arm or hip. They are used to dull the pain of contractions.

Before a woman is admitted to the hospital, she and her health-care provider should discuss the types of anesthetic. One anesthetic commonly used during labor is the epidural. Spinal anesthesia or general anesthesia may be used for a cesarean section.

Labor is another word for work—and delivering a baby is hard (but rewarding) work. Courses are available to help the mother understand labor and delivery. The mother should communicate her needs and feelings so her health-care provider and nurses can help her have a good experience of childbirth.

Delivery

During the birth, the baby travels out of the uterus, through the cervix, and into the vagina. The vagina stretches as the baby travels through it and out of the mother's body. The vagina is often called the birth canal, because canal is another word for passageway. When it is time to push, squatting or standing can sometimes help the mother use the force of gravity to aid in pushing. The mother does not have to push continuously. If she has had a baby before, or if this baby is small, the time needed for pushing may be very short. If this is her first baby or if this baby is bigger than her other babies, it will probably take longer.

The health-care provider may perform an episiotomy, a surgical incision to enlarge the vaginal opening. This procedure takes place just before the baby's head crowns to make space for the baby to

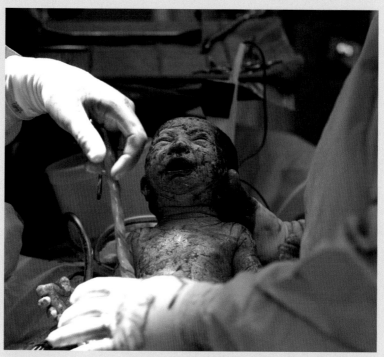

If at any point during the delivery the doctor feels the baby or the mother is in danger, she may call for a cesarean section. This is a surgical procedure done to remove the baby from the woman's uterus.

pass through. The first glimpse of the baby gives most mothers a final burst of strength to finish the delivery. Most of the time, the baby's head comes out first. A baby may arrive face up, but it is usually face down. Before delivering the rest of the baby's body, the health-care provider will make sure the umbilical cord is not wrapped around the baby's neck, then suction the baby's nose and mouth, and wipe the baby's face. The baby's head will turn, and the rest of the baby is delivered. A clamp will be placed in each of two sections of the umbilical cord, and then the cord is cut between the two clamps. If the mother or coach wants to help cut the umbilical cord, the mother should tell the health-care provider to let her know when it is the right time.

Sometimes the health-care provider uses **forceps** or a **vacuum** to help ease the baby out of the vaginal canal. These instruments are used when the baby's head is already in the vagina. This type of help is necessary when the mother is exhausted from pushing, or there is a need to speed up the delivery of the baby, or when a cesarean section is not immediately available.

After the umbilical cord is cut, the newborn is handed to a nurse or **pediatrician**, or placed on the mother's abdomen or in a crib. Babies do not have to scream loudly to be healthy. The baby's status is checked and rated. A few minutes after the baby is born, the placenta or afterbirth is delivered. If the baby is in good health, the mother will be given some time to spend with the baby right after birth. The mother may try to breast-feed, but some babies learn about breast-feeding along with the mother.

The moment has arrived when a mother and/or father can finally hold the newborn. Some parents will hold the baby as soon as it's born, while other mothers need time to rest first. But sometime soon, the new parents will begin holding, feeding, and touching the baby. And the baby will respond to voices, smell, and touch. Bonding has begun. For many women, labor and delivery are painful. For many women, this life-changing event is worth all the hard work.

Apgar score is a test developed by Virginia Apgar, a New York anesthesiologist. The heart rate, muscle tone, respiration, reflexes, and color are assessed one minute after birth and five minutes after birth. Each vital sign is given a score of zero, one, or two. A high Apgar usually means the baby is healthy and does not need further assistance. A low score indicates that the baby needs some immediate attention; for example, the baby might need extra breathing support.

Did you know?

- Miscarriages and **stillbirths** are more frequent among teens than among adult women.
- Teens under the age of fifteen have high rates of pregnancy complications.
- Teens are twice as likely to have premature infants.

Each labor is different. Generally, labor lasts longer for first-time mothers than for women who have already given birth. It could take twenty-four hours or only four hours. Once labor starts, a woman should not make any plans for at least forty-eight hours.

The Labor Coach:

- Helps the mother maintain proper breathing technique.
- Offers emotional support.
- Massages various parts of mother's body.
- Makes sure the mother is as comfortable as possible.
- Holds and coaches the mother while she pushes.

The baby's heart rate is monitored during labor. This can be done by attaching a monitor to the mother's abdomen or internally with a monitor. The monitor records the fetal heart rate and uterine contractions, and then records the results as a graph. Monitoring the fetus allows the health-care provider to track the baby's health.

Chapter 6
Life with Baby

Despite his dramatic entrance into the world, Holly's son Joey seemed to suffer no lasting ill effects. He weighed six pounds, two ounces, and was eighteen inches long. He also had a full head of dark, curly hair, just like his father. His mother and grandparents declared him to be the most beautiful thing they had ever seen, and Holly had left the hospital totally in love with her son.

Six weeks later, she still loved Joey, but the job of being his mother had left her frightened and completely overwhelmed. Holly had no idea what had made her think she could do this. Maybe Scott had been right all along; maybe she should have had the abortion. Maybe she should have put Joey up for adoption; at least then he would have ended up with a mother who knew what she was doing.

Little Joey had been screaming for the last hour and a half, and nothing she did seemed to comfort him. Weren't mothers supposed to have some sense or intuition about what their baby needed? What was wrong with her?

Walking the floor with her tiny son, Holly felt a wave of panic rising in her chest. She had fed him, burped him, changed his diaper, tried putting him in his swing, and had even taken his temperature. Everything seemed to be fine, and yet he was still howling. Holly had tried calling her mom at work for advice. Her mom had been great through Holly's pregnancy and during the first couple weeks after her surgery. Lately, though, Holly could tell that the strain of having an infant in the house was starting to get to her mother. Today must have been a rough day at the office because she wasn't very helpful when Holly got her on the phone.

"What is it now, Holly?" her mother asked irritably. "You know I've asked you not to bother me at work unless it's an emergency."

"It *is* an emergency, Mom! Joey won't stop crying, I've tried everything I can think of but nothing seems to work. I don't know what to do!"

"Babies cry, Holly. That's what they do. Now, my supervisor is giving me the evil eye for taking another personal call at work. You are Joey's mother. Being a mother isn't easy, but you'll just have to figure this one out yourself."

Since she had had no luck with her mother, Holly tried calling Joey's father for support. Scott hadn't been there for her much during her pregnancy, but since the baby's birth six weeks ago, he had come to visit a few times. The last time he said that if she needed anything, she could call him. Maybe he could come over and give her a break for an hour or so, just so she could get a shower and hear herself think.

She was pleasantly surprised when he answered his cell phone.

"Hey, Scott, it's Holly. Listen, Joey won't stop crying, I can't figure out what's wrong with him, and I think I'm going to lose it! Could you maybe come over for a little while and help me out, just to give me a little break?"

There was a moment of silence. "Uh . . . I'm sorta busy right now. I'm packing. School starts for me next week. Besides, what could I do, Holly? I don't know anything about babies. Can't you try your mom or one of your friends?"

Holly sighed. Her friends thought Joey was really cute, but they were always busy with summer jobs, parties, and boyfriends. There wasn't a lot of time left over for them to stop by and help out with babysitting or laundry. Holly had been expecting a lot more help. It was funny: she had thought that having a baby would be a comforting thing, that she would never feel alone again now that she had someone that really and truly belonged only to her. Instead, having a son had actually made her feel even more lonely.

Joey's face was bright red from crying. Frustrated and desperate, Holly began to cry with him. The baby shrieked with the frantic, rhythmic pattern of a newborn, drowning out the sound of Holly's own sobs.

Suddenly, she felt angry. None of this seemed fair. She should not have to be dealing with all this on her own. Where was her mother? Where were her friends? Where was Scott, who was supposedly so in love with her this time last year? Oh, right. He was going off to college like nothing ever happened! Joey's screaming grew louder, and Holly had a sudden urge to shake him hard and shut him up. The impulse scared her so badly that she very carefully laid him down in his bassinet and shut the door. In separate rooms, Joey and his mother cried themselves to sleep.

Holly felt a little better after her nap. Sleep was something she rarely got enough of these days. It was a good thing she had gotten some rest; she had lots of work to do. It was amazing that such a tiny person could create so much chaos!

First, Holly put in a load of wash, before unloading another load of Joey's tiny clothes from the dryer. She had to take the cover off his car seat and wash that too because he had spit up all over it. After getting all his clothes put away, she headed downstairs to the kitchen to wash some bottles.

Holly was starting to regret that she hadn't chosen to breast-feed. The bottles always seemed so gross to wash, especially if they sat in the sink and the formula started to stick to the sides. You had to use a special brush to clean out the nipples too. Plus, it was a pain to get up in the middle of the night and make a bottle. Sometimes, it would take her a while to get it made, and Joey would be screaming the whole time. He would get himself so worked up that by the time she did get it to him, he would try to swallow in huge gulps and get a belly full of air. Then she would spend the next two hours burping him while he cried some more.

Holly had had a hard time recovering from her cesarean delivery. It had hurt to walk, to breathe, even to laugh. She was supposed to avoid going up and down stairs, and was warned not to lift anything heavier than her baby. Her parents had been very helpful to her for the first week or so, but soon the whole ordeal began to wear on them. Having a baby in the house was definitely stressing out her parents, too.

One day, when Joey was about twelve days old, Holly had heard him crying upstairs. She knew her mom was up there, so she waited for her mother to go get him and bring him to her. After a few minutes, Holly's mom came flying down the stairs.

"What are you doing?" her mother snapped. "Why are you just letting him cry like that?"

"Well, I knew you were up there. I thought you would get him for me, you know, since it still hurts to go up and down the stairs."

"Holly, I told you from day one. This is your baby, not mine. Whether you're sore or not, tired or not, busy or not, from now on that little boy is yours to take care of. Now get up and go feed your son!"

Later, her mother had apologized to Holly for being so harsh, but Holly realized that her mother was sorry for how she had conveyed the message, not for the message itself. The baby was keeping everyone in the house up at night and affecting everyone's routine, creating short tempers all around. Holly noticed her dad had been staying away from home more and that seemed to be irritating her mother as well. Bottom line: this baby was Holly's responsibility, and her mother was expecting her to grow up enough to handle the load. But Holly wasn't sure she could.

She was also worried about school starting up again in September. She had thought about dropping out and getting her GED, but in the end, she had decided to go back to school. Her school had a program for teen mothers that would allow her to bring the baby to school with her and put him in day care while she was in class. She would have to spend her lunch break and any free periods down in the nursery, not only taking care of Joey but helping out with the other girls' babies. Last year, back when she was pregnant, it had all seemed like a good idea—but now, Holly was nervous about going back to her old school. She could barely find time to take a shower every day—how was she ever going to handle everything school would entail?

She had other worries as well. How would everyone treat her now that she was a mom? Would she ever be able to hang out with her friends again and feel normal? Now, whenever she talked to her closest friends, she felt separate from them. Things had happened to her that they couldn't understand. And all the things that were important to them, stuff that had been important to her too not so long ago, now seemed pointless and childish. She didn't care at all about who was seeing who or which song was going to be the prom theme. She was much more concerned about whether or not she had what it was going to take to raise a son alone.

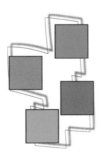

Bringing Home the Baby

Babies quickly learn the way to get what they need is to cry. But many babies cry a lot during the first month, whether they need something or not. Holding and cuddling is very important for babies. Being held close while feeding provides the feeling of warmth and closeness that the baby needs. A baby's feeding time is also pleasant and healthy for the mother. A newborn has very strong sucking muscles and a little pad of fat in each cheek to help it. The baby will suck on anything that is put near its mouth.

The first day or two after birth, the mother's breasts produce a liquid called colostrum. This yellowish substance provides both nourishment and antibodies

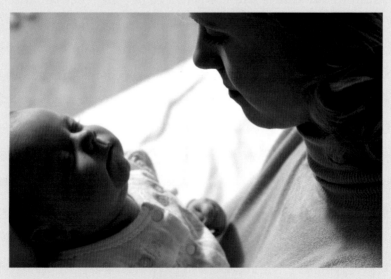

Adjusting to life with a new baby can be exhausting. The new mother will need enough sleep to stay healthy and capable. Therefore, she may have to learn to sleep when her baby is sleeping.

that help protect the baby from infections. When the baby is ready for more, the mother's breasts will become hard and engorged with milk. Even if a new mother does not breast-feed, her breasts will become engorged with milk. If she does not nurse the baby, the milk production will stop by itself within a few weeks.

Breast-feeding (also called nursing) is a learning experience for both mother and baby. Sometimes babies find it difficult at first to put his or her mouth around the nipple correctly. Many medical facilities have **lactation** experts, who are trained to help new mothers and their babies succeed at breast-feeding.

Bottle-feeding is a perfectly safe and healthy way to feed the baby for mothers who cannot or choose to not breast-feed. Many good mothers do not wish or are unable to nurse their babies. These babies are fed from a bottle that contains a special formula similar to breast milk, and they can grow to be strong and healthy.

When a mother and her baby are home from the hospital, the mother will discover the joy of parenthood can also be a time of adjustment and exhaustion. Sometimes newborns have their days and nights confused. A new mother may have to adapt as best as she can by sleeping when the baby sleeps. Rest is the key to good health and the ability to be a good parent.

The mother needs to recover physically, she will feel all types of emotions, and the baby will make constant demands. A new mother may find herself overwhelmed with all the chores that need to be done when she is by herself. Some mothers have a relative stay and help for the first few days. How much time a mother needs to recover depends on her experience during childbirth and how quickly her body heals. Some women feel well within a week or two after delivery, while others take months to feel fully

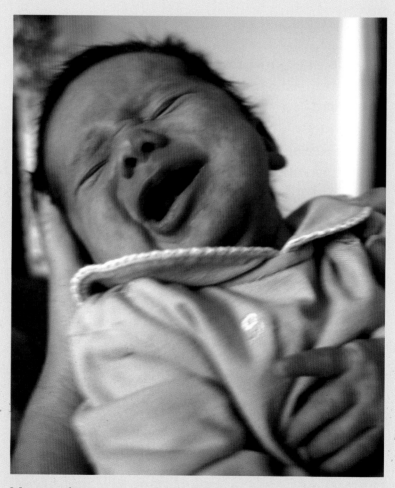

Many newborns cry a lot during the first month, even if all their needs are apparently met. It is normal for a new mother to feel overwhelmed by the crying, as well as by all of her new responsibilities.

recovered. If the mother had an episiotomy, it will take a few weeks or even months to heal completely. If she had a cesarean section, her abdominal incision will take quite some time to heal completely. After six weeks, the mother will return to her health-care provider for a checkup to make sure her body has completely recovered from childbirth.

A new mother should call her health-care provider if she has problems before her six-week checkup.

Problems such as:

- signs of an infection
- vaginal discharge becomes bright red or is foul smelling
- severe and persistent abdominal pain
- persistent fever
- any other unusual problems

Do not use breast-feeding as birth control. Ovulation and pregnancy can happen when a woman breast-feeds, even if she does not get her period. If a woman doesn't want to get pregnant when breast-feeding, she should use a safe contraceptive.

Getting Back to Normal

Q: When will I be able to fit in my old clothes?
A: Some women can fit in their jeans in a few weeks, but most women take several months. The more extra weight a woman gained during pregnancy, the longer

it will take to fit into her regular clothes. This is not the time to diet. To help lose the weight, she should exercise. Taking the baby for a brisk stroll every day is great exercise. Breast feeding also burns calories.

Parenthood

For teens, parenthood is especially difficult. They must give up their own childhood in order to put the baby first. Many teens are raising children with the help of family, friends, boyfriends, community programs, or alone. Many teen moms drop out of high school. These moms and their children may not have good prospects for the future. Some will end up on welfare. Because they have so little to look forward to in life, some teens choose parenthood even if it is not in their best interest. Parenthood is a life-changing event.

Most of us look forward to finding a life partner, someone with whom we can share the pleasures, responsibilities, and difficulties of family life. If a parent is going to establish a family with her partner, she may want to consider marriage. Marriage is a serious legal contract binding both partners. Each one accepts legal as well as moral and emotional obligations to the other. Every state has laws about marriage. A couple should consider premarital counseling. Having a child can bring joy, stability, and many other rewards to a relationship. A child can also strain the best relationship. If the commitment between partners is not solid, the relationship may fail.

Before someone decides to be a single parent, she should ask family and friends for their support. Even with support, single parenting is not easy. It is time-consuming and often complicated and frustrating. The parent can take great pleasure helping the child grow, but there will be no breaks. The child will constantly look to the parent for love and care. As the child's needs change, so will the parent's ability to meet those needs. If the child is ill or disabled, even greater effort may be required. It takes years for children to become responsible for themselves.

The parent may become more dependent on her family and friends, for help with the child, money, and

Parenthood can be difficult even for people who have planned for it. For teens, who must give up their own childhood to care for a baby, it is especially challenging.

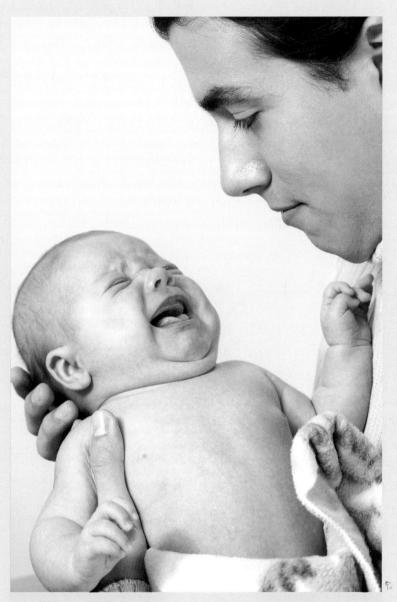

Not all teenage fathers desert the mother of their child. However, those that remain involved are likely to feel overwhelmed with their new responsibilities.

emotional support. The parent may have to give up a lot of freedom to be a good single parent. Parenting requires love, energy, and patience. A person must want to do this for a long time.

Babies are special, and most mothers and fathers love their babies. But it is usually easier and healthier for teenagers to wait until they are older to have a baby. It gives the baby and the parents a better chance to have a healthy start together. Some, but not all, teen fathers share these difficulties. Other teen fathers refuse to accept their responsibility and stay with their partners. Some men deny they are fathers. For a variety of reasons, sometimes the young women or their families reject the fathers' help or involvement. However, many young men do marry or live with their partners and babies and face these difficulties.

While the new mother is going through emotional and physical changes, the father will have his own problems. He may feel anxious. Some fathers feel hurt and left out. When those hurt feelings build up, the relationship can end up in trouble. Sometimes a father feels overwhelmed by the responsibilities of the new baby and will tune out and leave everything to the mother. The mother may soon feel abandoned if she has to care for the infant full time. The mother and father need to communicate their feelings to each other.

Chapter 7
Looking Ahead

No, Joey! You can't climb up the slide backward!" Holly ran over to the slide and scooped up her energetic, curly-headed toddler. "You're going to get killed out here some day, you know that!" The only response she received was a dimpled grin. Holly sighed, but she also couldn't help but laugh.

"Ice keem! Ice keem!" Joey pointed at an ice cream truck approaching the playground.

"I know. Ice keem. Come on, let's get you some." Holly took Joey's chubby hand in hers and set off for the ice cream truck to buy a Popsicle.

Sitting in the shade of a large willow as Joey licked his Popsicle, Holly thought about how hard the road had been that had led her to this point. She hadn't been able to handle high school and Joey at the same time, so she had quit right before Christmas the year he was born. She was too tired to concentrate in class, she didn't have time for homework, and she never felt like she was a real part of the school anyway. So she dropped out. The following summer, once Joey started sleeping through the night so she could get a night's sleep too, she had earned her GED certificate.

Her parents weren't happy, though, when she dropped out of school, and they had demanded that she get a job if she was going to continue living with them. Holly finally got hired as a companion for an elderly lady who had had a stroke. It turned out to be a perfect job for her, since the work didn't require any special skills. The older lady loved having a baby around the house again, so Holly didn't have to pay for day care.

Best of all, she and Mrs. Becker had formed a strange kind of friendship. The old woman's husband had died years ago, leaving her a widow at twenty years old with two small children to raise. She sympathized with Holly's struggles as a young single mother, and the two women bonded. It was funny, Holly had often thought, but she had more in common with an old lady than she did with girls her own age.

When Mrs. Becker died about a year ago, Holly was grief stricken. Not only had she lost a close friend, someone she had come to rely on for understanding and emotional support, but she had also lost her source of income. As she tried to figure out what her next step would be, she was surprised when Mrs. Becker's daughter called and invited her and Joey to join her for lunch.

"My mother thought very highly of you," Susan Becker told Holly. "You and Joey brought a lot of joy to her last few months."

"Thank you." Holly wasn't sure what else she could say, except the truth. "I really loved your mother. It was a shame she had to pass away when she did. I would have liked Joey to have been able to know her better." Tears filled her eyes. "I had imagined her being like a second grandmother to him."

Susan smiled. "Well, my mother left something for you. It's not much, but I know she wanted to see you pursue your education. A few days before that last stroke, she told me, 'There are a few old savings bonds in the box under my bed. If anything happens to me, make sure you cash them in and give some money to Holly. Tell her to put it toward going back to school.' I did just as she asked." Susan slid a bank envelope across the table to Holly. "There's about seven hundred dollars in there. It's not much, but it should pay for a couple semesters' worth of books."

Holly stared down at the envelope. "I don't know what to say. I don't think I can go to college, I mean I dropped out of high school. It was just too much for me." She pushed the envelope back toward Susan. "You should probably keep the money. With my son and everything I don't know if I'll ever get back into school."

Susan shook her head. "Listen, lots of women are single parents. It doesn't mean you can't go to college. Our community college accepts people with GED certificates all the time, and you could probably get financial aid to help you with tuition, living expenses, maybe even day care. Don't give up on yourself, Holly. You have too much potential."

In the end, Holly accepted the money with gratitude. Susan was right: it wasn't enough to really make much difference financially—but somehow it made all the difference in the world that Susan and her mother had believed in her enough to give her the money. Holly made an appointment to meet with an admissions counselor at the community college.

To her amazement, Mrs. Becker's daughter had been right. The school had a lot of money available to single parents. They even had their own day-care facility right on campus. With Holly's SAT scores, the school was happy to accept her, regardless of the fact that she had a GED instead of a "real" diploma. Suddenly, for the first time in years, Holly was excited about the future.

The only problem was deciding what to study. For some reason, becoming a veterinarian didn't hold the appeal for her that it once had. All her experiences having Joey, and all the people who had been willing to offer Holly help now made working with people seem much more rewarding to her than working with animals. Looking at a list of the school's available programs, she saw that it would only take her three years to become a registered nurse.

Nursing seemed like a natural choice to Holly. Throughout her pregnancy, she had been cared for by nurses every step of the way. She had also enjoyed taking care of Mrs. Becker. Plus, she was always interested and asked lots of questions when she took Joey to the pediatrician. Nursing school felt like a good fit.

Going back to school made a tremendous impact on Holly's emotional well-being. She finally had a chance to socialize again, and although most of the people she met were a little older, she found she had more in common with them than she did her friends from high school. Like herself, many of her fellow students were working, or raising children, or both.

One of the other students she met was a guy named Greg. He was two years older than her, and he also had a son, Zachary, who was three. Holly and Greg had two classes together. One day, he asked her if she wanted to grab lunch after biology class, and to her surprise she had said yes. They hit it off, and soon they were spending most of their free time together with Joey. Holly's favorite times were the weekends when Greg had Zachary and all four of them could be together.

Meanwhile, Scott had never really been involved in Joey's life. Occasionally, he would stop by to see Joey if Scott was home from college for a break, but mostly he sent Holly one hundred dollars every month and stayed out of the picture. As Holly got to know Greg better, she was glad to realize that not all guys were like Scott. Greg took his responsibilities to his son as seriously as Holly did to hers—and she could tell that Greg loved Zach as much as she loved Joey.

Lots of other exciting things were happening in Holly's life at the same time. The financial aid she got from going back to school included a stipend for living expenses. That meant that once she got a part-time job waiting tables, she could afford her own place. The day she moved into her own one-bedroom apartment with a little fenced-in yard out back was one of the best days of Holly's life. She and Joey spent a sunny Saturday morning planting flowers for a small garden. Actually, she did most of the planting while he made piles of dirt in various sizes and poked a couple of earthworms. It was still a very satisfying way to spend a morning.

Holly's relationship with her parents also improved dramatically once she had her own place. For the first time in a long time, Holly felt like her parents were proud of her. Instead of being a high school dropout, their daughter was a college student, a single parent with a job and her own home. Holly knew she had earned her parents' respect. She also knew that she couldn't have done any of it without their help.

Sitting under a tree on a sunny day with her son, Holly realized how many good things there were in her life that she couldn't have imagined three years ago when she found out she was pregnant. She had been able to access programs to provide her with good prenatal care, helping her have a healthy baby. She was a confident mother, having completed several parenting classes. She had been able to find baby supplies, nutrition classes, healthy food, and financial assistance to help her complete her education. It hadn't been easy, and a lot of it hadn't been much fun. And it had taken all the support that her family and her community could offer. In the end, though, Holly realized with pride, she had transformed herself from a teen in crisis to a thriving member of society.

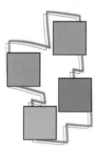

Pregnancy and School

Research has shown that being pregnant and going to school present many challenges. Many young women decide to drop out of high school—but if an adolescent mother decides to stay in school, research indicates that she's likely to graduate, despite the difficulties.

Research studies yield the following statistics about teen mothers:

• Thirty-two percent of adolescent mothers complete high school by the time they reach their late 20s, compared with nearly 73 percent of women who delay childbearing until after they're twenty-one.

Unfortunately, statistics show that teenage mothers are less likely to finish high school than women who wait to have children. However, if a teen mother does decide to stay in school, studies show that she is likely to graduate.

- About 40 percent of all adolescent mothers who drop out of high school attain a **GED certificate** by the time they're thirty.

- Young women who begin childbearing after age twenty are much more likely than teenage mothers to attend college.

- Adolescent fathers are less likely to graduate from high school than older fathers.

- Children of teen parents perform worse in school than children of older parents. They are 50 percent more likely to repeat a grade, perform significantly worse on developmental tests, and are more likely to drop out of school.

Parenting and Employment

Failure to complete high school often prevents young mothers from going on to postsecondary education and from participating in many vocational training programs—and this often means fewer employment opportunities and lower wages for teenage mothers.

Research studies indicate these statistics are true:

- One-fourth of teenage mothers have family incomes below the poverty level, compared with less than one-tenth of those who delayed childbearing.

- Adolescent fathers earn, on average, $4,732 less annually than those who delay fathering until age twenty-one, and are therefore not as prepared to contribute financially to the well-being of their families.

- Nearly 30 percent of children born to adolescent mothers are neither working nor looking for work nor attending school by

Though a teen parent is not without hope of a successful future, she will face more obstacles to her success than other teens. If she makes the decision to keep her child, a teen mother must be prepared to work hard to beat the odds.

the time they are twenty-four years old, in contrast to 17 percent of children born to mothers who have delayed childbearing.

Choosing to raise a baby doesn't mean a young person is destined to be poor, or that his or her child will not do as well as others. Plenty of young people have what it takes to beat the odds. But all teen parents need to carefully consider the challenges they will face before making their decisions.

Having a baby when a person is too young can be difficult. Some babies have health problems at birth and as they grow up. Parents often find it hard to care for a baby, especially if they are young teenagers themselves. The teen parents often lose the freedom to do what they want. They find it hard to go out with friends or to get schoolwork done when a baby is around. Teenagers who have babies often drop out of school because they need to work. It may be difficult for teenagers to get a job to pay for food, clothes, toys, and medicine for the baby. The cost of paying someone else to take care of a baby while the parents go to school or work is an additional stressor.

Bringing a baby into this world is an important and exciting event. Becoming a parent is one of the biggest changes that can happen to a person. Caring for and loving a child can be a wonderful and amazing experience. It brings with it all sorts of new and different responsibilities. That is why the decision to start a family is so important. Parenting is a lifelong commitment.

Glossary

abstinence: Restraint from indulging a desire for something, such as sex.

forceps: Surgical instrument resembling tongs or tweezers.

GED certificate: A high school equivalency certificate; general educational development.

genitals: The reproductive organs, especially the external sex organs.

incontinence: The inability to control urination or defecation.

lactation: The production of milk by the mammary glands.

pediatrician: A physician who specializes in the care of babies and children.

prenatal: Before birth.

puberty: The stage of development when individuals become physiologically capable of sexual reproduction.

quickening: The stage at which fetal movement can be felt.

speculum: A medical instrument used to hold open a body passage.

stillbirths: The delivery of dead fetuses after the twenty-eighth week of pregnancy.

vacuum: A suctioning device.

zygote: A human egg that has been fertilized by a sperm.

Further Reading

Curtis, Glade E., and Judith Schuler. *Your Pregnancy Week by Week (Fourth Edition)*. New York: Perseus Publishing, 2000.

Douglas, Ann. *The Mother of All Pregnancy Books*. New York: Wiley, 2002.

Eisenberg, Arlene, Heidi E. Murkoff, and Sandee E. Hathaway. *What to Expect the First Year (Revised)*. New York: Workman Publishing Inc., 2003.

Eisenberg, Arlene, Heidi E. Murkoff, and Sandee E. Hathaway. *What to Expect When You're Expecting (Revised)*. New York: Workman Publishing Company, Inc., 2002.

Lees, Christoph, Karina Reynolds, and Grainne McCartan. *Pregnancy and Birth: Your Questions Answered (Updated Version)*. New York: DK Publishing, Inc., 2002.

For More Information

Adoption.com
www.adoption.com

Advocates for Youth
www.advocatesforyouth.org

All About Moms
www.allaboutmoms.com

America's Crisis Pregnancy Helpline
800-672-2296
www.thehelpline.org

The Center for Young Women's Health, Children's Hospital Boston
www.youngwomenshealth.org/healthinfo.html

Childbirth.org
www.childbirth.org/articles/preglinks.html

National Family Planning and Reproductive Health
Association
www.nfprha.org/facts/contraception

Obstetric Ultrasound
www.ob-ultrasound.net

Planned Parenthood Federation of America, Inc.
www.ppfa.org/health

Pregnancy Hotline
800-848-LOVE
e-mail: nlc1st@snit.net

Project Reality
www.projectreality.org

Safe Place
www.safeplaceservices.org/teentopics/sex.shtml

SHARE (Sexuality, Health, And Relationship Education)
www.share-program.com/teen.htm

Teen Health
www.medill.northwestern.edu/journalism/newmedia/
Capstone/Group3/index.htm

TeensHealth
kidshealth.org/teen

Publisher's note:
The Web sites listed on these pages were active at the time of publication. The publisher is not responsible for Web sites that have changed their addresses or discontinued operation since the date of publication. The publisher will review and update the Web-site list upon each reprint.

Bibliography

Alan Guttmacher Institute. "Recent Statistics, Policy Papers, and Reports on Teen Sexual Behavior, Pregnancy and Birth." http://www.agi-usa.org/index.html.

Campaign for Our Children. "Facts and Statistics About Teen Pregnancy." http://www.cfoc.org/Home.

Cherry, A. L., M. E. Dillon, & D. Rugh (eds.). *Teenage Pregnancy: A Global View.* Westport, Conn.: Greenwood Press, 2001.

Child Trends. "Adolescent Sexual Behavior and the Teen Birth Rate." http://www.childtrends.org.

Kids Count. "When Teens Have Sex: Issues and Trends." http://www.aecf.org/kidscount/teen.

Michigan Department of Community Health. "Health Risk Behaviors: Teen Pregnancy." http://www.michigan.gov/documents/TeenPregnanciesFeb00_10428_7.pdf.

Planned Parenthood. "Pregnancy & Childbearing Among U.S. Teens." http://www.siecus.org.

Planned Parenthood. "Reducing Teenage Pregnancy." http://www.plannedparenthood.org/pp2/portal/files/portal/medicalinfo/teensexualhealth/fact-teen-pregnancy.xml.

Urban Institute. "Involving Males in Preventing Teen Pregnancy: A Guide for Program Planners." http://www.urban.org/Template.cfm?NavMenuID=24&template=/TaggedContent/ViewPublication.cfm&PublicationID=5921.

Index

Picture Credits

cc-by-sa 2.5/Chris 73: p. 19
Corbis: p. 86
istock.com
        Paternoster, Marcos: p. 88
Jupiter Images: pp. 35, 66, 69, 100, 102, 106, 116, 118
Medisphere:p p. 59, 72
Photodisc: pp. 33, 62
Stockbyte: pp. 60, 105

To the best knowledge of the publisher, all other images are in the public domain. If any image has been inadvertently uncredited, please notify Harding House Publishing Service, Vestal, New York 13850, so that rectification can be made for future printings.

Authors

Heather Docalavich has written several books for young people on a variety of different topics. She is a single mother of four children and lives in South Carolina. Her experiences with her own children have given her tremendous respect for teen mothers and their unique challenges.

Phyllis Livingston has degrees in both special education and psychology. She has counseled teen mothers in a variety of settings.

Series Consultants

Cindy Croft, M.A.Ed., is the Director of the Center for Inclusive Child Care (CICC) at Concordia University, St. Paul, MN. The CICC is a comprehensive resource network for promoting and supporting inclusive early childhood and school-age programs and providers with Project EXCEPTIONAL training and consultation, and other resources at www.inclusivechildcare. org. In addition to working with the CICC, Ms. Croft is on the faculty at Concordia University and Minneapolis Community and Technical College.

Dr. Pam Burke is a certified family and pediatric nurse practitioner with a doctorate in developmental psychology. She has worked in maternal and child health nursing for almost four decades, combining clinical practice, teaching, and research in the area of adolescent pregnancy and parenting.

(4a)